TECHNIQUES of UPHOLSTERY

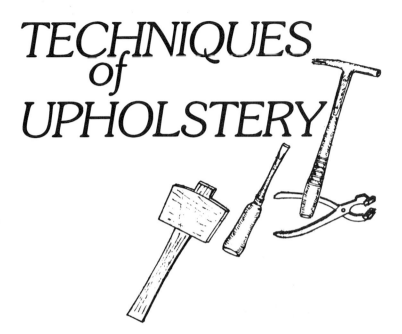

Dining and Bedroom Chairs and Stools

by
Robert James McDonald

BT Batsford Limited London

To the memory of
my beloved wife
Anne

ISBN 0 7134 5356 7

Typeset by Katerprint Typesetting Services Limited, Oxford
and printed in Great Britain by
The Bath Press Ltd
Bath, Somerset
for the publishers
B. T. Batsford Ltd.
4 Fitzhardinge Street
London W1H 0AH

Contents

Introduction

This handbook is the first of a series of four books containing detailed explanations of both traditional and modern methods of upholstery progressing from simple upholstery projects through to the more advanced and more difficult forms of the craft. These handbooks have been written for the student, apprentice, craftsman and amateur alike.

The purpose of producing four separate handbooks is to grade the various upholstery projects more easily into convenient sections, and to describe more fully and clearly the various details and processes involved in upholstering any particular item. It also allows for a wider field of upholstery work to be covered.

The aim of these handbooks is to make it possible for the reader to select the volume which includes the particular upholstery work he or she wishes to undertake. Hitherto, most books on upholstery adopted a general approach to the subject and had a limited coverage of specific projects.

I would like to mention, in passing, that over years of teaching the craft, I have found that women have had great success with upholstery and I would be delighted if these handbooks encouraged more women to try their hand at upholstery projects.

A glance at the list of contents or the index will enable the reader to ascertain which of the handbooks in the series contains the particular item for which the reader requires information. If the exact item is not included, he should follow instructions for something which is very similar, where details may be somewhat alike and may be adapted.

I hope that readers of this book will get absorbed in the subject and have their appetites whetted so that they will undertake further upholstery projects, either in restoration and repair, or new work. I have spent my working life dealing with upholstery in production and teaching fields and have always found the work fascinating and the craft a very satisfying one. The years spent teaching students and young apprentices have been invaluable in assessing the type of information and instruction to be conveyed.

One of the prime requirements in undertaking any upholstery task is ample patience. It is important not to be in too much of a hurry to complete the work. Always remember that the amateur has to live with the results of his or her mistakes which are often the result of impatience. If the work looks unsatisfactory or unsightly, you will always regret not having taken a little more time on the job and a little more care.

Throughout this book reference will be made many times to 'temporary' tacking or fixing of materials, etc., in the first instance. This is a vital stage which cannot be passed over. Even the most skilled professional will 'temporary' tack materials at certain stages, then check and observe if the material or covering fabric is lying straight and square upon the item being worked. This is not just a waste of time or doubling-up of the process. It is true to say that many amateur upholsterers do not realise the importance of this stage – with the result that they often achieve a disappointing finish to the work. Very rarely can one lay a piece of woven cloth on to a stuffed, or even flat, piece of upholstery and find that the weave of the cloth is running exactly parallel with sides, front and back edges, which is the ultimate aim for a professional-looking finish.

Materials

A problem which many amateurs undertaking upholstery work frequently find most difficult to cope with, other than the work itself, is locating a source of supply of upholstery sundries or materials with which to carry out the work. This is not too great a problem with modern upholstery materials where one is replacing perhaps resilient rubber webbing or renewing foam cushions or foam filling for seats and backs, etc., as most of these commodities are available at larger D.I.Y. stores or even at small local shops.

Other types of supplies which may be used for refurbishing a traditionally upholstered piece are rather more difficult to track down. You may need linen or jute webbing, hessian (canvas), different sizes of coil springs, fillings such as fibre and horsehair and a variety of other bits and pieces, including tacks of different sizes.

To assist the reader with this problem, this handbook contains a useful list of addresses of suppliers of upholstery sundries, spread throughout the country. These traders should be able to supply the enthusiastic amateur with most items in small quantities. Unfortunately, wholesale suppliers to the upholstery manufacturers will not sell the items on a small scale.

The reader will, no doubt, appreciate that rampant inflation continues to affect prices of goods; the upholstery sundries supply is no exception. There has been, over the years, a continuous increase in prices but, of course, doing the work for oneself will offset the high cost of materials.

Figure 1 shows a range of tools normally used by the upholsterer using traditional methods of upholstery.

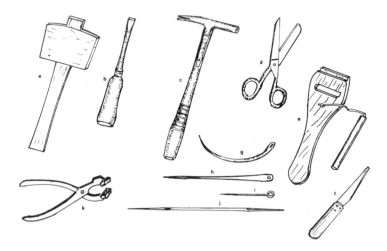

1. Upholstery tools: **a** mallet, **b** ripping chisel, **c** upholsterer's hammer, **d** scissors, **e** webbing stretcher, **f** leather knife, **g** spring needle, **h** regulator, **i** skewer, **j** bayonet needle, **k** hide strainer.

Tasks

This handbook deals with a variety of items especially selected for the person who may not have attempted upholstering tasks before. All the tasks are within the scope of the novice. By following the instructions given in this book, there should be no difficulty in obtaining a professional appearance which can be so rewarding. Some items will be found to be more difficult than others and it would be best (if the reader can choose or if he/she has a number of items to upholster or re-upholster) to undertake the simpler jobs first to get the 'feel' of working with soft flexible materials on a small scale.

Most beginners may find that it is a little difficult, initially, to work with wood or metal which has to be shaped by using a tool of some kind. It is generally easier to work with 'soft' materials which need to be formed by touch and manipulation and which have to be sculpted.

Dining chair seats

There are many hundreds of styles of dining chairs using many different methods of seat upholstery. Bearing in mind that all furniture is produced in different price ranges, it is generally the case that some seats may be upholstered rather sparsely to conform to a low selling price, whilst at the other end of the price range, there will be well-upholstered chairs conforming to a high standard of craftsmanship – even with today's rising costs, a demand for excellence exists.

Generally, to produce upholstery at a competitive price, most dining chairs are mass-produced and are mostly made in the form of a separate unit such as a loose 'drop-in' seat, or a flat board which has been thinly padded with foam and covered with fabric and then screwed to the main base frame. This is illustrated in figure 2. The method of upholstery is described on pages 7 to 13. A typical 'drop-in' type of seat frame is shown in figure 3. A number of options are available in ways to upholster these seats and it is possible to change from one method to another in the process of re-upholstery if desired. Various different methods are described from pages 14 to 53.

Included in this book is a section describing the upholstering of chair seats 'fully' upholstered in the true traditional manner using horsehair and fibre fillings with edges stitched into rolls (*figure 41*).

This type of upholstery is rather more specialized than that described earlier but genuine antique chairs will originally have been upholstered in this manner so must be refurbished in the

2. Popular style of dining chair with upholstered seat

3. Dining chair detachable seat with plywood support

same way. A number of period reproduction chairs are produced with sprung seats but, strictly speaking, the earlier seats were 'top' stuffed, that is, without springing within the seat, the stuffing and stitching being on the top of the seat frame (*figure 4*).

4. Webbing on a 'top-stuffed' chair seat

FLAT PLY BASE SEAT (*Figure 2*)

MATERIALS

Foam: 1 piece 50 cm (20 in) square × 2.5 cm (1 in) thick; firm density. This measurement can be adjusted to suit the size of the seat, purchasing slightly oversize to allow for cutting to the shape of the seat.

1 piece 30 cm (12 in) square × 1.2 cm ($\frac{1}{2}$ in). This is to create a slight doming effect.

Fabric: 60 cm (24 in) front to back of the seat × 60 cm (24 in) side to side – again these sizes can be adjusted to suit the seat base size. The measurement side to side normally would be approximately half the width of the roll of upholstery fabric, or slightly less, thus two seats may be cut across the fabric width which would be approximately 122/127 cm (48/50 in).

It must be stressed that only stout fabric suitable for upholstery use should be used; dress fabrics in this situation tend to wear and soil quickly.

Tacks and staples

As the baseboard for the seat is made from rather thin plywood or other fabricated board, tacks used for fixing the covering material to the underside of the board should be no longer than 10 mm ($\frac{3}{8}$ in) using either the 'fine' or 'improved' variety. 'Fine' upholstery tacks in all sizes infers that they have a slender shank with a head which is smaller than the 'improved' type; the latter also have a slightly thicker shank. There are certain stages in upholstering where the latter may be more useful.

There is a wide range of sizes of tacks used for upholstering. A professional upholsterer would probably have most of the range to hand, kept handy in little bags or pockets attached to his working bench so that he can switch easily from one size to another. This is a very convenient arrangement if one is making frequent use of tacks.

Caution must *always* be exercised to ensure that tacks do not penetrate through the timber into which they are being hammered and emerge on the upper side. Also, of course, a further important aspect is not to use a tack so large that it will split the wood. Quite frequently it will be observed that the larger tacks, 16 mm ($\frac{5}{8}$ in), will in many cases split a fairly light sectional rail on part of the seat or chair frame.

Sizes of tacks normally available to the professional craft upholsterer engaged in the traditional style of tacking are: 10 mm ($\frac{3}{8}$ in), 13 mm ($\frac{1}{2}$ in), 16 mm ($\frac{5}{8}$). Fine and improved types are available in each of these sizes (*figure 5*). There are longer sizes made but avoid these as they are unsuitable for upholstering purposes.

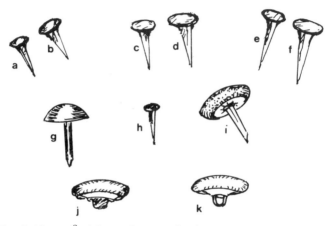

5. **a/b** 10 mm ($\frac{3}{8}$ in) fine and improved tacks,
    c/d 13 mm ($\frac{1}{2}$ in) fine and improved tacks,
    e/f 16 mm ($\frac{5}{8}$ in) fine and improved tacks, **g** oxidised decorative nail,
    h gimp pin, **i** covered stud, **j** covered button with tuft,
    k covered button with wire loop

It is doubtful if the average local D.I.Y. store would be able to supply the full range mentioned but you should be able to find two or three types of tacks which will be suitable for most work.

Tools and adhesives
An alternative to using tacks for attaching coverings and other materials is the use of strong wire staples using a stapling hand gun. The normal wire staples used for stapling papers together do not have the strength to penetrate wood. When punched into the wood they will fold or the legs will break off.

Should you intend to undertake a number of upholstering jobs, it would be worthwhile investing in a good strong staple firing gun (*figure 6*). This would fire 10 mm ($\frac{3}{8}$ in) and 6 mm ($\frac{1}{4}$ in) staples.

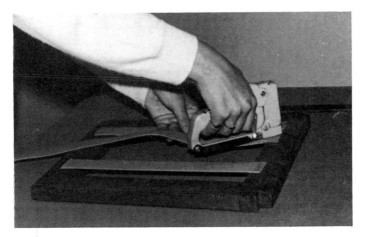

6. Using a hand staple firing gun

A good sharp pair of scissors is the only other tool required to do the actual upholstering of the seat. Before any upholstery can take place the old covering and filling must be removed from the seat. It is extremely unwise to cover over an existing cover. It is far better to take the trouble to remove the soiled and, possibly greasy, old material and to renew the filling within.

An adhesive suitable for sticking the foam to the base board will be needed and this need only be applied around the outer perimeter, say 5 cm (2 in), from the outer edges.

It is as well to remember when using foam filling in any upholstering work that it should be anchored to prevent 'creep', that is, any movement from its original position. It will tend to ride over an edge after a period of use, giving an unsightly line.

Stripping old material and filling
Generally, with this modern type of chair seat the covering fabric will have been stapled into position on the underside of the base

board. These staples may well be sunk into the covering (especially if the covering is rather thick) and particularly so if a powerful compressed air staple gun has been used, so they may be a little difficult to remove.

The professional upholsterer would have a special tool handy for removing difficult staples but, of course, the amateur would not have access to such a tool. The next best tool to do this job would be a sharp screwdriver with a narrow blade. By pressing the blade firmly into the fabric under the cross bar of the staple, it is an easy matter to prise the legs out of the timber. There is, of course, an important safety rule to observe whilst doing this which is *always* to work away from your body and not to hold the seat with the other hand in front of the screwdriver blade. This is to ensure that in case the tool slips, there is no danger of injury to yourself.

Alternatively, an upholsterer's regulator (*figure 7*) is often used to remove staples. Any other strong, pointed instrument may be used, but again, this must be done with care.

Once the covering has been removed, the interior filling will be exposed. This may be some form of cotton shoddy filling in sheet form or may be polyurethane foam (plastic foam). Whichever it is, the filling should be removed and discarded. Any filling

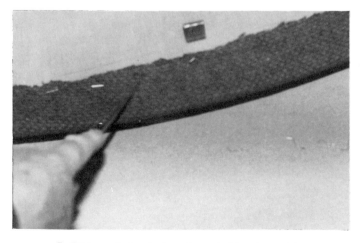

7. Prising out wire staples using upholsterer's regulator

still adhering to the board must be completely removed so that you have a clean start.

Upholstering the seat

The foam you have purchased may be in a large sheet to be cut into a number of seat pieces, or it may be in individual pieces. This foam must now be cut to size. Lay the seat board upon the thicker of the two pieces, draw around the outer line of the board using a felt tip pen (a biro line is hardly visible). This outline should be a firm and plainly visible line. The foam may be cut with a sharp knife with a long, broad blade (*figure 56*). The foam should be cut fractionally oversize, say 0.5 cm ($\frac{1}{4}$ in) outside the drawn line as this will allow for any slight shrinkage of the foam whilst working. The foam will cut better if the knife is drawn upwards in long firm strokes rather than with a sawing action.

The thinner and smaller piece of foam which is to be used to give a slight doming effect should be cut so that it is approximately 10 cm (4 in) smaller all round. After cutting to size, a taper or bevel should be made by cutting with sharp scissors on the four sides (*figure 8*). This should then be stuck in the centre of the seat. The bevelled edge is placed under the larger piece of foam and stuck to the baseboard with the bevelled edge face down so that there is no upstanding thick edge.

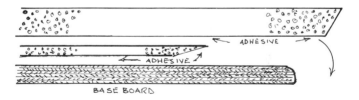

8. Section through plywood base seat showing bevel of smaller foam insert

When sticking the larger piece of foam on to the board, adhesive need be put only in a narrow band around the upper surface of the board. Ensure that the foam is located accurately with the slight over-cut protruding equally around each edge.

Covering should be cut so that there is ample to fix to the undersides. In some instances, with this style of chair, the main rails around the top of the chair frame may hide the tacks or staples used to hold the covering when the seat is fixed into position. Assuming you have two, or perhaps four, seats to cover, if you fold the full width of covering in half and cut along the half width line, this should give sufficient covering for two seats with ample to fold underneath the seat for fixing.

The procedure in fitting the covering is in the first instance to make a pencil or biro mark on the underside, at the centre of the seat board front and back. Do the same with the cut covering on its front and back edges so that you can check whether the fabric is correctly centered.

Lay the fabric on the foamed-up seat; having carefully centered the covering, lift the seat and covering on its side edge and with 10 mm ($\frac{3}{8}$ in) tacks, *temporary* tack first the front edge, then back edge, then either side. Temporary tacks should be hammered into the wood just sufficiently to hold so that they may be removed easily and quickly.

Having observed your work at this stage and checked that the weave of the fabric is lined up with the front and back and sides, the temporary tacks should be tapped away progressively so that any slackness may be smoothed across the surface of the seat easing the loose material out under the seat and then fixing by tacks or staples. When covering over foam filling, the fabric should

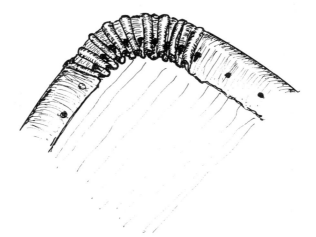

9. Pleating covering at a radius corner

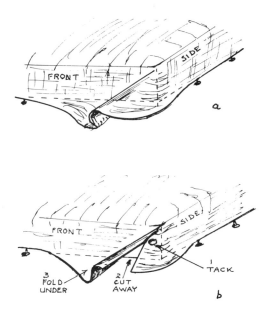

10. **a** and **b** Pleating covering at a square corner

not be *over-strained* so that the foam is flattened – it is just the loose wrinkles that need to be smoothed away. Do not hesitate at the temporary tacking stage to re-position the covering if you feel it is not straight. Ensure that the tacks or staples holding the covering finally are hammered 'home' fully. If a finger is run along the line of tacks or staples it becomes apparent if any are protruding.

Should the seat have radius corners, the covering should be tacked in the centre of the radius in the first instance, then work in each direction from the centre to form small pleats by easing the material gently and tacking after each pleat. Figures 9 and 10 show pleating at a radius and a square corner. Corners should be attempted only when the front, back and sides are fixed.

For an extra neat finish to the underside of the seat a piece of matching lining or some black fabric may be attached, folded under and tacked leaving a narrow border of covering showing, approximately 1 cm ($\frac{3}{8}$ in) around each edge.

THE 'DROP-IN' LOOSE SEAT

EXAMPLE 'A'

As mentioned earlier, there are a variety of methods used in upholstery of the dining chair 'loose' seat. Figures 11 to 14 show some of the more common methods.

Re-covering a seat is a fairly simple matter if the interior filling and frame are sound but, for our purposes, we will strip and completely re-upholster some of the examples shown. It is likely you will find the particular example you have chosen to work on amongst those shown.

The first stage is to prepare your work area. Stripping off old upholstery from a timber frame is rather a dusty and messy job. If possible, you should do the work in the garage or shed. Should you have to do the job in the house, lay a cover over the carpet to catch the old tacks or staples and other debris, and find an old unpolished table to work upon. On no account should you work on a polished table as this will ruin the polished surface. If an old table is not available, lay a thick covering, such as a blanket, over the surface and take care that tacks do not find their way under it. This will also have the advantage of preventing the frame from slipping around.

Tools

No specialised tools are absolutely essential to undertake this work; there are substitutes for the tools normally used by the profes-sional. Instead of an upholsterer's hammer any lightweight

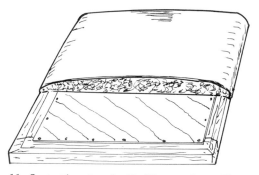

11. Seat with cotton shoddy filling on plywood base
EXAMPLE 'A'

14

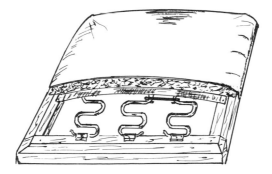

12. Seat with cotton felt filling on sprung base
    EXAMPLE 'B'

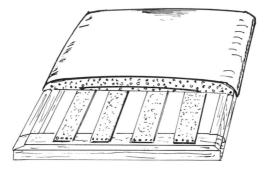

13. Seat with foam filling on resilient rubber webbing base
    EXAMPLE 'C'

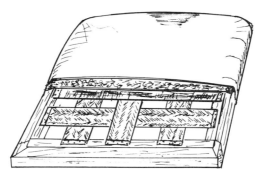

14. Seat with hair filling on linen webbing base
    EXAMPLE 'D'

hammer with a smallish face will do. Alternatively, a staple firing gun may be used providing it is heavy duty. It is very important to have a good pair of *sharp* scissors; the larger they are, the better. The upholsterer's ripping chisel may be replaced with an old screwdriver. The handle of the screwdriver may get damaged, so I suggest you do not use your best one. Instead of the wooden mallet to be used with the screwdriver, you can use a hammer with a larger face than the one we will be using for tacks. If staples have to be removed, an upholsterer's regulator, which is often used for the job, may be replaced by some other tool you may already have, with a long, strong point.

If linen or jute webbing is to be used, you will need a webbing strainer to tension the webbing or, alternatively, a piece of wood may be used as shown in figure 15a/b.

15. **a** Alternative to using
upholsterer's webbing tool

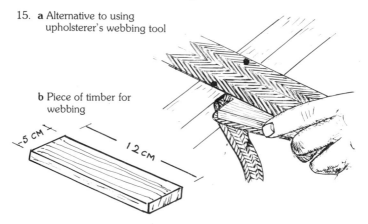

b Piece of timber for
webbing

·5 CM

12 CM

Stripping off old covering and filling

To remove the old tacks, use the ripping chisel or old screwdriver, with the blade held alongside the head of the tack to be removed. Pressing down firmly into the material it is holding, give the end of the tool two or three sharp taps with the mallet or hammer and the blade should force itself under the head of the tack so that it may be prised out of the wood. It is important to work *with* the grain of the wood, that is, to knock the tacks out parallel with the sides (*figure 16*). Working across the grain will often chip pieces off the sides leaving a bad edge. It could even split the timber which would

16. Hammering tack out *with* the 'grain' of the timber

mean unnecessary extra work in repairing it. Many seats have an undercover tacked around the bottom. This will have to be removed before the tacks or staples can be removed from the covering material.

Try to remove all the old tacks or staples. There may, however, be an obstinate two or three which refuse to budge. Do not risk damage to the frame. Instead, just hammer them well 'home' into the wood after pulling the fabric free so that they do not stand proud. As a safety precaution it is advisable to rub a piece of coarse glasspaper over the area from which the tacks have been removed to remove the short splinters which are invariably left in the process of pulling out tacks. There is no need to fill in the holes left by the tacks.

Upholstering *(Example 'A')*
Starting with the simplest form of upholstery, example 'A' (*figure 11*), we will assume we are to undertake a complete renovation of the seats. As figure 3 shows, the support for the filling is a piece of thin plywood nailed to the top edges of the frame. This may be found to be damaged. For instance, if it has been stood upon to

reach a high cupboard a heel may have penetrated the plywood. This will need replacing before upholstery can commence. If replacement of plywood is necessary, it is as well to consider taking the plywood off completely and replacing it with webbing and hessian (canvas). Using webbing, hessian or even replacing the plywood with rubber resilient webbing can make a seat much more comfortable. If either of these courses of action is decided upon, the instructions for figures 13 and 14 should be followed.

When fitting a new piece of plywood, before nailing it down on to the frame, ensure that the top outer edges are sanded down with glasspaper to form a bevel so that there will be no ridge left to feel through the filling.

MATERIALS

A piece of foam 2.5 cm (1 in) thick (minimum) of firm density slightly larger than the seat frame size so that the outline of the seat may be drawn upon it with a felt tip pen. A sharp bread knife can be used to cut the foam. The foam should be cut a little oversize by allowing approximately 0.5 cm ($\frac{1}{4}$ in) extra around the outside of the line you have drawn; this will allow for any shrinkage of the foam whilst working.

A small amount of adhesive will be required for applying on the foam, as well as some 10 mm ($\frac{3}{8}$ in) tacks or staples.

Covering fabric should be of a good upholstery quality. It is possible to cut two seats from a 122/127 cm (48/50 in) width by folding the fabric in half and cutting down the centre line. For the measurement front to back, take a tape measure and allow approximately 4 cm ($1\frac{1}{2}$ in) for tacking underneath at the back. Then bring the tape measure over the surface of the foam and allow 4 cm ($1\frac{1}{2}$ in) again under the front edge. If four seats are to be covered, this measurement should be doubled, so four seat covers will be obtained from just the two measurements back to front (*figure 17*).

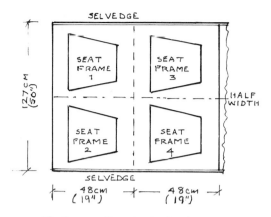

17. Cover cutting plan for four loose seats

Upholstering the seat

After cleaning off any splinters or uneven surfaces from the seat frame, mark the centre point of front and back rails on the underside of the frame with a pencil. Do the same with the covering so that the centre of the fabric may easily be lined up with the centre of the seat frame.

Cut the foam as described earlier and remember to allow the slight oversize amount. Having cut round the outline, cut one of the surface edges to form a bevel so that it forms a taper on all four sides (*figure 29*). The cut bevel should be placed on the underside when fixing the foam into position. Spread adhesive around the under faces of the foam approximately 6 cm ($2\frac{1}{2}$ in) in width and place carefully on the surface of the seat pressing down all round – it will assist the sticking process if the edges are weighted down. Allow a short time for the adhesive to set. If the foam is not stuck down properly, it will tend to creep away from the edges during use.

Covering

The covering of the seat has to be done with a certain amount of care. Firstly, the thickness of the new covering should be compared with the one which has been removed from the seats. Should the new material be a good deal thicker it will mean that the seat will

19

not fit into its housing rebate without some adjustment to the seat frame.

It is a good idea to cut a small strip of the new fabric and fold it in half so that you have a double thickness. Then holding the two layers of fabric against the edge of the seat attempt to slide the seat into the rebate. The object of using the two thicknesses is that they represent the actual thickness of the covering on both sides of the frame (*figure 18*).

18. Testing clearance of 'loose' seat for new covering

If it is found that the seat frame will not fit with the new material it is a fairly easy task to rub a piece of coarse glasspaper along the edges to ease down the sides of the seat frame. If a large amount needs to be taken off, a wood rasp or a surform tool will do the job quite quickly.

Conversely, if the new covering is a good deal thinner than the original, an unsightly gap between the sides and front and back edges will show. There is a simple solution to this problem. Before starting to apply the covering, cut strips of stout cardboard of equal width to the edges of the seat frame and tack as many of these along the edges as are required to get a perfect fit with the thickness of covering (*figure 19*). You may need one or two thicknesses depending upon the thickness of the card and the gap to be filled.

Start the covering process by placing the piece of fabric which has been cut for the seat over the surface of the foam allowing an equal amount of surplus on all sides. Then carefully, without disturbing the positioning of the fabric, stand the seat on its

19. Cardboard tacked along edge of seat

rear edge on the work table holding the fabric in position as you do so. Fold the covering over the front edge, making sure that the centre marks align. Put one temporary tack on the centre marks to hold the covering, then smooth the covering towards the corner and put in another temporary tack about 4 cm ($1\frac{1}{2}$ in) from the corner. Do the same on the other front corner. Once the corners are fixed in position put another temporary tack between the centre and side tacks so that there are five tacks along the front edge. Figure 20 shows the sequence of temporary tacking.

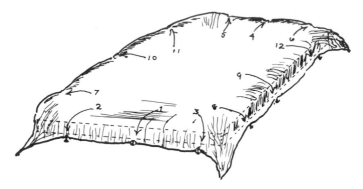

20. Numbered sequence for temporary tacking covering

Reverse the process of temporary tacking, described above, for the underside of the rear of the seat. This time, rest the seat on its front edge, and follow the same sequence using the same number of tacks. The same process is repeated on each side so that the covering is held in position on all four sides with five temporary tacks. Should the seat be tapered towards the rear, as some are, the temporary tacking along the sides should be started at the front corners smoothing the covering towards the rear corner whilst tacking.

Having temporary tacked with the tacks only partly hammered into the wood frame, check the covering for straightness. The weave of the fabric should be parallel with the front and back edges except for a slight running off at corners where the filling will be a little thinner. If the position of the covering is satisfactory, starting at the centre, tap each temporary tack away in turn as you hammer home fresh tacks to replace them, hammering the fresh tacks completely home with a spacing of approximately 3.5 cm (1½ in). Whilst hammering in the fresh tacks, smooth the covering towards the corners to work the fullness out into the pleat at the corner. Leave the corner pleats until the covering is tacked home on all four sides. The method for pleating the corners is shown in figure 10a/b. The pleats should be folded on the two front and back corners.

On completion of the covering operation the seat should finally be fitted into the rebate housing in the main chair frame. On no account force the seat into the rebate; it should be a sliding fit. If you do force it there is a high risk of opening up the joints of the chair frame and making it unstable. If you have previously tested the double thickness of the new covering as suggested earlier, and found there is no tightness, then it is possible that the pleating of the corners has not been done properly. The fold of the pleat and the material underneath is too bulky.

You will note in figure 10b that a section of the covering which has been pleated is cut away. If there is difficulty in fitting due to thickness of the corners, lift out the tacks holding the pleat and endeavour to remove a little more material from underneath the fold. Having done that, lightly hammer the tack and the covering as flat as possible without damaging the material.

A final task which will give a neat and tidy appearance to the underside of the seat is to tack or staple a piece of lining, calico or even hessian, over the base to cover the raw edges of the top covering which should have been tacked approximately 2 cm (1 in) from the outer edges of the frame.

This bottoming material should be folded *under* and attached on the four sides leaving a border of covering material (approximately 1–1.5 cm $(\frac{1}{2}-\frac{5}{8}$ in) on each side) showing. The tacks or staples being used should be placed on the extreme edge or fold of the bottoming fabric so there is no risk of the folded edge lifting and curling up to spoil the neatness of the finish.

SPRUNG LOOSE SEAT

EXAMPLE 'B' (*Figure 12*)
Generally, a dining chair loose seat is fairly flat and thinly up-holstered. To enable manufacturers to produce a sprung seat giving slightly more resilience than example 'A' which had a ply-wood base, a departure is made from the traditional coil spring (*figure 21*).

This type of springing is known as 'serpentine' or 'sinuous' springing. Some popular trade names are 'No-Sag' and 'Zig-Zag'. There are also other trade-mark names.

Because sinuous springing is used in comparatively short lengths in this type of seating it does have minimum flexibility. Nevertheless, when this springing is used there is a marked differ-ence in comfort as compared to the hard plywood seat. Also, a

21. Sinuous springing of 'loose' seat

slight doming effect given to the finished article tends to make the seat look more comfortable and inviting.

These springs are fairly durable but they have one failing in particular – the metal clips fixing the last loop to the frame (*figure 22*) may fracture or the nail holding the clip may lose its head or work itself out of the timber, thus allowing the particular strand to become free. If either of these things happen it is easy to spot; the spring length will curl back upon itself and show below the base of the seat (*figure 23*). Each strand, if released, will form itself into a small circle. Fortunately this is fairly easily remedied whilst re-

22. Metal clip to hold sinuous spring

23. Result of broken nail from clip fixing spring

upholstering. Otherwise, you can perform an emergency repair following an alternative method of fixing the strand of springing back into position. Usually it is only one strand that will need attention.

MATERIALS

Replacement hessian (canvas), good quality, 46 cm × 46 cm (18 in × 18 in) per chair seat. Check this size with the seat you are dealing with; make a slight extra allowance for tensioning (with your hands) and for a fold over when tacked – the size mentioned here will suffice for most seats.

Hessian is supplied in either 91.5 cm (36 in) or 183.0 cm (72 in) widths. If you are able to purchase 183.0 cm (72 in) width, 4 seats can be cut across the full width of hessian, or, if 91.5 cm (36 in) is bought, 2 seat widths will be obtained from it. Thus, if the seat requires 46 cm (18 in) back to front, purchasing that amount across the full width of hessian will give either 2 or 4 pieces of the size required, depending upon the available width.

Interior filling: In some instances the original filling may be re-usable, such as cotton flock which will be in layer form and in good condition. If the filling needs discarding, it may be replaced with a good, firm density foam. 46 cm × 46 cm (18 in × 18 in) will normally fit but check this measurement, particularly if your example is a 'carver' or 'elbow' chair, as these are often larger across the width of the seat.

Lining or calico, 46 cm × 46 cm (18 in × 18 in) to be used as an undercover.

Covering fabric: An average size chair will require 51 cm × 51 cm (20 in × 20 in) upholstery quality fabric which is normally 122 cm/127 cm (48/50 in) in width. If you buy 0.5 m (20 in) across the full width, the fabric will suffice for two seat covers.

Lining, calico or hessian for bottoming for the seat 46 cm × 46 cm (18 in × 18 in).

13 mm ($\frac{1}{2}$ in) and 10 mm ($\frac{3}{8}$ in) fine tacks.

Simulated leather covering, P.V.C., expanded vinyl and polyurethane coated fabrics are all purchased by the lineal measurement as is soft fabric. The width of the simulated leather cloth is normally greater than that of woven soft fabric; it is usually approximately 137 cm (54 in), or can be wider. Calculating the quantity of cloth needed is the same as for woven soft fabric. Simulated leather is somewhat wider but two seat covers only may be cut from the width.

Stripping old upholstery and repairing springing
Let us assume that we have a faulty spring which has come adrift from its fixing in a seat and is curling out on the underside of the seat, or bulging through the bottom of the chair seat, and we have decided to completely re-upholster.

   With the ripping chisel and mallet or old screwdriver and hammer, carefully remove the tacks or staples holding the bottoming material. Remember to hammer the ripping tool in the direction of the grain of the timber to avoid damage to the seat frame. At this stage you can see if the springs are in order or whether they need attention.

Remove the covering material which will be tacked on the underside of the four sides. Lifting the seat frame off the worktop away from the loose covering should allow the filling to fall away from the hessian covering the springing. The hessian will, no doubt, be in poor condition and need replacing. Remove the hessian by hammering the ripping tool against the head of the tacks. These tacks may be longer than those used to hold the covering and may be more difficult to remove. It is a great temptation to tear the hessian away from the tacks in order to get the work done more quickly. It is best to remove the tacks in the conventional manner for a clean professional approach.

Should there be a faulty spring clip it would be apparent at this stage. You may find that the head of the nail or nails holding the clip and spring in position has broken off. If this is the case a new 2.5 cm (1 in) nail will hold it in place again. Should the clip be fractured, causing the spring wire to come adrift, fix it back into position using a short length of upholstery webbing folded double to attain the correct width around the last bend of the spring. Tack it down into position (after removing the remnants of the broken clip) with 13 mm ($\frac{1}{2}$ in) tacks. 2.5 cm (1 in) good, strong quality curtain heading tape (used double) would also be satisfactory. Help may be needed to hold the spring down into position whilst tacking. The tacks should be put into the webbing or tape as close as possible to get a tight fixing and to avoid the possibility of the wire slipping out from the webbing or tape whichever is being used (*figure 24*).

With all the springs now in sound condition, the seat frame should be cleaned of any protruding splinters by rubbing a piece of coarse glasspaper over the surfaces. Any tacks remaining which are too difficult to remove without damage to the frame should be hammered 'home' absolutely flat.

Upholstering
Some examples of dining chair loose seats may well be shaped, or curved, across the width (*figure 24*). In this instance it must be remembered that the curve must be maintained in the upholstering process. Endeavour not to straighten the surface line of the upholstery on the seat. Whilst applying hessian, filling and covering

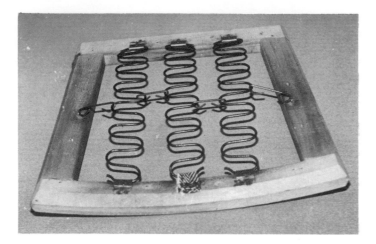

24. Spring held back in place with webbing

fabric, the main tensioning of the materials should be back to front only, with just sufficient easing across side to side to remove fullness or wrinkling.

First, hessian should be tacked on to the top side of the seat frame over the springs. Start tacking working from the centre point with the hessian folded *over* so you have a double thickness across the front rail. It is convenient to work with this front rail furthest away from you with the hessian lying loosely towards you over the seat. Using 13 mm ($\frac{1}{2}$ in) or 10 mm ($\frac{3}{8}$ in) improved tacks, tack at the centre, then towards the ends of the front rail at approximately 3 cm ($1\frac{1}{4}$ in) spacing. With the front tacked, tension the hessian towards the back rail, which is closest to you, as firmly and tightly as possible with the fingers, starting to tack once again from the centre point towards each corner. In this instance, tack the hessian on the single thickness – do not cut surplus away yet. Tack single thickness along each side rail. If the seat is narrower at the rear, start tacking the hessian from the extreme front and work towards the back of the seat. If the seat side rails are parallel you should start tacking from the centres again. With the hessian now tacked on the four sides (one side folded), trim away the surplus hessian leaving approximately 2 cm ($\frac{3}{4}$ in) to be folded and tacked on the remaining three sides. We now have the four sides reinforced with double hessian.

Should the original filling be re-usable, this can be laid over the springs carefully without disturbing the layer and making it uneven. However, it is possible that the filling may feel a little skimpy. If this is the case, and you wish to increase the depth of filling, a layer of Terylene 'Fibre-fill' may be laid over. 'Fibre-fill' in sheet form may be purchased in many fabric or drapery stores, it has excellent resilience and may be purchased in small quantities.

The loose layered filling and 'Fibre-fill' may be rather difficult for the inexperienced to cope with. The beginner may not be able to control the filling around the sides and edges. Therefore, (as allowed for in the materials list) it is wise to put on an undercovering over the filling before attempting to tack or staple on the final covering fabric. A thin lining or a cotton calico will be suitable for this.

Before applying the undercovering, neaten the filling around the sides, back and front of the seat. It is imperative that no filling should be allowed to work down around the edges of the frame. If this is allowed to happen, the covered seat will *not* fit into the chair rebate.

Applying the undercovering

Figure 20 shows the best method of applying undercovering and the top covering fabrics – both must finish with no visible looseness or wrinkling with the weave of the fabric running perfectly straight front to back and side to side. Weave lines running parallel with the front and back edges (side to side) will run off a little at the extreme corners due to doming of the seat.

Sequence of tacking and tensioning of the fabric: for temporary tacking use 13 mm ($\frac{1}{2}$ in) or 10 mm ($\frac{3}{8}$ in) tacks:

1. Mark centres on front and back seat rails on the underside.
2. Lay calico/lining undercover over the surface of the seat which should be lying flat, top uppermost, on the worktop. Ensure that there is an equal amount of surplus material on all four sides.
3. Proceed using instructions as on pages 19 to 23 for covering Example 'A', using the same instructions both for the undercovering and top covering fabrics.

In this instance where we are using an undercover, it is wise to test the fit of the seat into the main frame rebate with a sample of top covering (*figure 18*) after the undercovering stage has been completed as the undercovering does add a little extra thickness to the sides and may affect the final fitting of the seat.

Particular care should be taken with pleating the corners using an undercovering. Pleats should be as thin as possible. It is an advantage to pleat or fold the undercover on the opposite side of the corner to that of the top covering, i.e. if top covering is pleated or folded on the face of front and back rails of seat, then undercovering is better folded on side faces of the corner. This will reduce the possibility of bulkiness preventing a good fit into the rebate.

Bottoming material can now be applied after establishing that we have done a satisfactory job, using 10 mm ($\frac{3}{8}$ in) tacks.

Use of simulated leathers

Simulated leather covering requires rather more care in fixing into position than most materials. It is important to check when turning the work over on its face on the worktop that there are no stray tacks lying upon its surface as these could severely scratch or even puncture the covering. This problem is not so apparent when using a soft fabric covering. On the other hand, it could easily ruin a P.V.C. or expanded vinyl covering, possibly even to the extent that a fresh covering may be needed.

The inexperienced may find more difficulty working with a plastic coated material than with a soft fabric. Fabric tends to be more flexible and it is easier to remove any 'fullness' or wrinkling that occurs than is the case with P.V.C. It is, therefore, even more essential that the temporary tacking and final tacking sequence described in figure 20 is followed. Putting tacks or staples into the seat in a haphazard manner will cause many problems.

If the original seat had a fabric covering which is now to be replaced with a plastic coated fabric, check the fit of the seat with a strip of double thickness of the new covering into the chair rebate. P.V.C. and suchlike materials are normally thinner than most fabrics so the edges of the seat frame may well need packing with card as mentioned earlier if an unsightly gap is to be avoided around each side of the seat frame.

LOOSE SEAT USING RESILIENT RUBBER WEBBING

EXAMPLE 'C' (*Figure 13*)

An alternative method of suspension for the filling for a loose seat frame is to use resilient rubber webbing providing the seat frame is structurally sound. Rubber webbing may be used to replace any other method of upholstery used previously on the seat; it is easily obtained at most D.I.Y. stores and very easy to use. The usual type sold at most D.I.Y. stores is manufactured by Pirelli Ltd. and is to be recommended. The webbing acts as a flat spring and will give a degree of flexibility to the seat.

The webbing is normally available in two widths 3.8 cm ($1\frac{1}{2}$ in) and 5.1 cm (2 in) in several colours although for normal work, in which the webbing is covered, it is usual to use the putty-coloured webbing.

Figure 13 shows a normal-size loose seat with strands of webbing fixed in position. Unlike traditional jute or linen webbing which is attached in both directions and interwoven, rubber webbing in this instance is applied in one direction only and applied fairly closely, leaving narrow gaps between the strands. There are occasions when this webbing needs to be interlaced. This aspect and the technique will be discussed later in the series.

It is better to use the narrower of the two widths of rubber webbing if possible, although the wider width may be used if it is the only available one. Four strands of the narrower webbing should be used front to back or, if using the wider type, three stands would suffice.

MATERIALS

Rubber webbing: 4 strands × 3.8 cm ($1\frac{1}{2}$ in) 1.40 m per seat.

Foam: 46 cm × 46 cm (18 in × 18 in) per seat including allowance for cutting × 2.5 cm (1 in) thick + 23 cm × 30 cm (9 in × 12 in) × 1.5 cm ($\frac{1}{2}$ in) thick per seat.

Undercover of lining or calico: 46 cm × 46 cm (18 in × 18 in) per seat.

Covering fabric: use good quality cloth suitable for upholstery covering. There will be more tension on covering with the use of rubber webbing.

An average size seat will require 51 cm × 51 cm (20 in × 20 in), similar to our previous examples, cutting the full width along the centre fold will give two seat covers out of the full width of fabric (*figure 17*).

Lining, calico or hessian as a bottoming for the seats 46 cm × 46 cm (18 in × 18 in).

Tacks or staples 10 mm ($\frac{3}{8}$ in) and 13 mm ($\frac{1}{2}$ in).

A small amount of adhesive suitable for sticking plastic foam.

4 strips of lining, calico or other similar material 46 cm (18 in) long × 5 cm (2 in) wide per chair.

Upholstery

With the seat frame completely cleared of all signs of earlier upholstery and old tacks, ensure that the rubber webbing is applied to the *top* surface of the seat. This should be apparent; in most instances the seat frame will have a long bevel or slope on the top surface so that the outer edge of the timber is narrower than the inner edge.

It is wise to mark with pencil or biro on the top surface of the frame positioning of the webbing. Assuming 3.8 cm ($1\frac{1}{2}$ in) wide webbing is to be used, the two outer strands of webbing should be approximately 2 cm (3/4 in) from the inside of the side rail (if the seat tapers to the back); reduce the 2 cm ($\frac{3}{4}$ in) to 1 cm ($\frac{1}{2}$ in) when tacking on the back rail. Then space out the two inner strands so that there is equal spacing between – there will be approximately spacing of half the width of the strand of webbing. Having marked this spacing it is now easier to proceed.

It is important that each strand of webbing should be tensioned to give it resilience and each strand should be tensioned equally. Tensioning amount to aim at in this instance is $7\frac{1}{2}$%, that is, the length of webbing actually used between the front and back rails is $7\frac{1}{2}$% less than the actual untensioned webbing. This is relatively easy to calculate, i.e. working with the rear of the seat nearest you, using 13 mm ($\frac{1}{2}$ in) tacks, tack the first strand in position; use single thickness with no fold over. Use four tacks and ensure each tack is hammered straight and with its head flat upon the webbing. Tacks with heads bent over will cut into the webbing and weaken it. With the webbing laid across the seat front to back, mark with pencil on the surface of the webbing the point where the inside of the rear rail meets the webbing. Now measure the distance *in between* the front and back rails and calculate $7\frac{1}{2}\%$ of that distance, i.e. if the seat measurement between front and back rails is, say, 26 cm ($16\frac{1}{4}$ in), $7\frac{1}{2}\%$ of that measurement would be 1.95 cm ($\frac{3}{4}$ in). Now mark with pencil this amount on the webbing in towards the centre of the seat; this is the amount the webbing needs stretching; the second line should reach to the inner edge of the frame when tacked (*figure 25*).

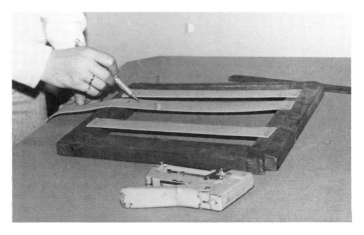

25. Marking rubber webbing to attain correct tension

Tensioning to this small degree is quite easily done with the hand without recourse to a web stretcher as with the traditional woven webbing. It is best to work the two outer strands first, then the two inner strands. Do *not* cut off each strand length separately before you start as it will be difficult to tension the webbing with short ends and it tends to be wasteful. Work one strand at a time working from the length you have available and then, when tensioned and tacked, trim off the remaining length with a sharp knife or scissors approximately 1 cm ($\frac{1}{2}$ in) from the tacking position.

There may be some difficulty in getting the seat to remain flat upon the worktop whilst tensioning the webbing. If a helper is not to hand to assist in keeping the seat steady, either place a heavy object on the opposite side of the seat to which you are working, or tack a short piece of webbing or other strong material around the frame and on to the worktop (not if it is a polished surface, of course). The looped holding piece can be moved along if it interferes with positioning of the webbing, and removed completely after the webbing process is completed.

Preparing foam filling
Rest webbed seat frame upon the surface of the thicker of the two pieces of foam. Mark around the outer edges of the frame with a felt tip pen drawing good, firm lines. Using a long sharp knife, cut slightly oversize, 0.5 cm ($\frac{1}{4}$ in) outside the line, aiming to get a good, square upright cut).

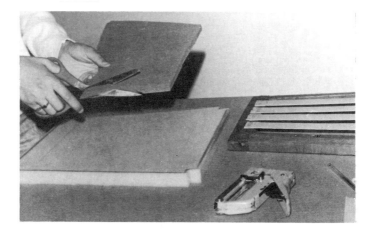

26. Tapering edges of smaller inset of foam

Now cut the smaller and thinner piece of foam to the same shape as the larger piece but cut it so that the two side edges will rest approximately in the centre of the two side webs. The front and back edges of this piece should reach the approximate centres of front and back rails. This piece of foam is used to give a doming effect to the seat and to add depth to the foam over the rubber webbing. However, it is not required right up to the outer edges of the seat.

Taper the edges of this smaller piece making a rather long bevel as in figure 26. Mark the position of this piece on to the surface of the larger piece so that the marking coincides with the position mentioned in the previous paragraph.

Now stick the smaller foam to the main larger piece accurately placing it on the lines drawn on the surface. The adhesive should be applied in a band around the four sides approximately 3 to 4 cm ($1\frac{1}{4}$ to $1\frac{1}{2}$ in) wide, applying adhesive also along the bevel. The bevelled side is the side which must be stuck down so that, when in position, there is no upstanding thick edge. This doming piece should be stuck to the underside of the larger piece. Then cut off the sharp edges of the main piece of foam on all four sides on one face only. This should be the face on which the extra piece is added. You do not need too much of a bevel – just a small amount to thin the outer edges a little (*figures 27, 28, 29*).

Using the four strips of thin lining or calico, apply a band of adhesive along each of them, approximately 2 cm ($\frac{3}{8}$ in) wide along one of the two long sides. Apply a band of adhesive the same width around the edges of the prepared foam and press the fabric firmly on to the surrounds of the foam so that it gives a flange for fixing the foam on to the seat. Do *not* be tempted to omit this stage, or the next of undercovering. It is very difficult for the inex-

27. Applying adhesive to tapered edges

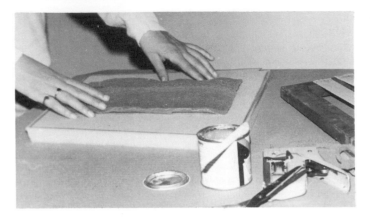

28. Sticking inset of foam into position

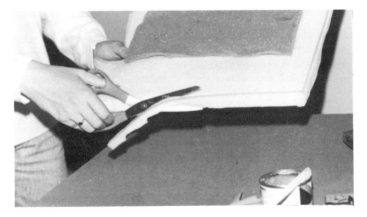

29. Cutting bevel edges on main foam

perienced to manage these materials properly so as to be able to control and shape the foam to ensure that it stays in position and to avoid any overlap of foam at the edges. Allow the adhesive to dry.

Fixing foam
Temporary tack the foam into position using 13 mm ($\frac{1}{2}$ in) tacks to hold the flange on to the edges of the frame on all four sides;

four or five tacks at this stage will be sufficient. When you are satisfied that the foam is positioned satisfactorily, fix the fabric flanges permanently using smaller 10 mm ($\frac{3}{8}$ in) tacks and ensure their heads are hammered home completely flat. Surplus fabric of the flange should be cut away from around the base of the frame and any surplus at the corners must also be cut away to avoid any bulk in the cover pleating area.

Undercover and covering
At this stage, test the fit of the seat in the rebate of the main chair frame using a sample of the new fabric to be used as covering (*figure 18*). If there is any packing card needed, it may be tacked on at this stage. Conversely, should it appear that the seat will be too tight to fit comfortably, the offending sides should have the flanges lifted and the required amount of frame removed.

When a satisfactory fit has been achieved, mark centres on undersides of front and back rails, also centre mark the under-covering. This should have ample surplus for handling whilst tensioning and tacking. Lay undercover over surface of seat whilst it is lying flat upon the worktop. Ensure that there is an equal amount of surplus on all sides. Lift up seat on its rear edge and temporary tack the undercover along the underside of the frame, lining up the centre marks on front rail first, turning the seat so you can do the same with the back rail and then the side rails. After temporary tacking, check for straightness of weave and if satisfactory, complete the undercovering process by hammering home flat 10 mm ($\frac{3}{8}$ in) tacks, with a spacing of approximately 2.5 cm/3.0 cm (1 in/$1\frac{1}{4}$ in). The temporary tacks should be removed progressively along each side.

Covering and undercovering should not be unduly tensioned; tension it just sufficiently so that there is no obvious looseness over the surface. A good test is by placing palms of two hands flat upon the surface of the seat at the side edges whilst the seat is lying top uppermost on the worktop. Then with quite light pressure rub the two hands towards the centre. Tensioning should be such that no looseness is pinched up to form a fold when the hands meet in the centre. Folding that pleat at the corners should be done on the other side of the frame to that where the covering is to be pleated.

30. Stapling covering on underside of seat

For tacking the covering into position follow the tensioning and tacking sequence given in figure 20, and for the pleating of corners follow instructions shown in figures 10a/b.

A nice neat finish is attained by tacking on a bottoming fabric, such as lining, calico or even hessian. This should be folded *under* with 10 mm ($\frac{3}{8}$ in) tacks placed on the extreme edge of the fold; space tacks approximately 3 cm ($1\frac{1}{2}$ in) apart. The seat should finally be a nice sliding fit into the rebate of the chair frame.

TRADITIONAL UPHOLSTERING OF LOOSE SEAT

EXAMPLE 'D' (*Figure 14*)

The traditional method of upholstery for a dining chair loose seat is probably the most satisfying test of craftsmanship and skill for the novice. It calls for rather more expertise and ability to handle materials than the previous examples so far described.

It will generally be true that a good genuine antique or a good quality reproduction chair or chairs will have been upholstered in this way so in order not to diminish the value of such chairs, they should be refurbished, when necessary, with the same type of materials and the method of upholstery.

The first thing you will notice is that the chair or chairs have a number written on the front of the seat on the bottoming material on the underside of the seat. The same number should appear on the front rail rebate, etched into the timber. This is usually done with a ripping chisel blade being hammered on to the wood. Numbers are usually 1 to 4 or 1 to 6 depending upon how many chairs are in the set. The numbers are to ensure that each seat frame is fitted into the rebate of the correct chair frame. Earlier chairs were mostly made by hand and seats were individually fitted. It may be found that some seat frames will not fit other chairs in the set. When the seats have been refurbished, the correct number should appear upon the new bottoming material and placed onto the correct chair.

Stripping seats

1. Strip off bottoming from underside of seat taking care to strip out tacks from the frame along the grain. The wood in earlier period chair seat frames will be dry and brittle and damage can easily be caused by careless stripping down. Any damage or splitting caused will have to be repaired before re-upholstery.
2. Strip off covering fabric. If the covering is to be replaced, ensure tacks are lifted out carefully without damage to the fabric. As the tacks are eased out of the wood remove them completely from the material and put them aside.
3. Lift off the cotton wadding which should be immediately under covering.
4. Strip off undercovering of cotton calico or lining. This may be tacked on the four edges of the seat frame which makes the job of stripping the undercover rather more difficult and the frame prone to damage.
5. With the undercover removed, the horsehair filling will be exposed. This will be held in place with twine ties sewn across the base hessian. Cut the twine in a number of

places and the filling should then lift off in a complete layer.

6. The supporting hessian (canvas) should have a line of tacks on a fold over around each side. Lift out with the stripping tool and hammer, first the tacks on top of the fold, then the tacks on the single thickness under the fold.

7. Webbing is now exposed. This will probably be black and white striped linen webbing, or brown-coloured jute webbing. The webbing too will be folded at the end of each strand but only half the strands will have tacks under the fold at both ends (*figure 31*).

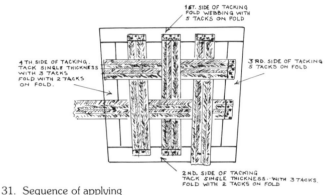

1ST. SIDE OF TACKING FOLD WEBBING WITH 5 TACKS ON FOLD

4TH SIDE OF TACKING. TACK SINGLE THICKNESS WITH 3 TACKS FOLD WITH 2 TACKS ON FOLD.

3RD. SIDE OF TACKING 5 TACKS ON FOLD

2ND. SIDE OF TACKING TACK SINGLE THICKNESS WITH 3 TACKS. FOLD WITH 2 TACKS ON FOLD

31. Sequence of applying woven webbing

8. Clean off any protruding splinters of wood. Hammer home any odd tacks which refuse to budge and repair any damage caused during the ripping process. Ensure that all joints in the seat frame are sound and that there is no movement at the joints.

Normally loose seat frames are constructed using dowelled joints but occasionally you will find, particularly with the older period chairs, that mortice and tenon joints are often used (*figure 32*). Should either of these types of joints be loose, the rails should be knocked apart, the old glue cleaned away and the frame re-glued together using a sash cramp to close the joints and hold them whilst the glue is setting (*figures 33 and 34*).

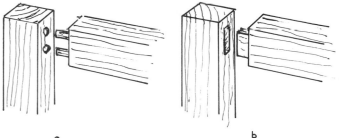

32. **a** Dowelled joint   **b** Mortice and tenon joint

33. Cramping joints together using 'sash' cramp

34. Using patented form of cramping device as substitute
for sash cramp

MATERIALS FOR 1 SEAT AND 4 SEATS
Quantities are approximate, to nearest convenient measurement:

1 SEAT	4 SEATS
Linen or jute webbing 2 m (2¼ yds)	8 m (9 yds)
Hessian (12 oz quality) 46 cm × 46 cm (18 in × 18 in)	1/2 m × 72 in width (1 yd × 72 in width)
	or 1 m × 36 in width (1 yd × 36 in width)
Hair filling 0.35 kg (¾ lb)	1.40 kg (3 lbs)
Calico underlining 46 cm × 46 cm (18 in × 18 in)	46 cm × 72 in width (18 in × 72 in width)
	or 1 m × 36 in width (1 yd × 36 in width)
Covering fabric 46 cm × 24 in × ½ width (18 in × 24 in)	1 m × 48 in width (1 yd × 48 in width)
Bottoming fabric 46 cm × 46 cm (18 in × 18 in)	1 m × 72 in width (1 yd × 72 in width)
	or 2 m × 36 in width (2 yds × 36 in width)
Skin wadding 46 cm × 36 in width (18 in × 36 in width)	2 m × 36 in width (2 yds × 36 in width)
10 mm (⅜ in) tacks	
13 mm (½ in) tacks	
Flax twine	

TOOLS

      Light hammer
      Webbing stretcher (or substitute)
      Pair of scissors
      Curved needle (large semi-circular) to take twine

Reupholstery – webbing

Webbing used for traditional style upholstering is supplied in two types, i.e. black and white striped herringbone made from linen and cotton fibre, normally 5 cm (2 in) width, and jute webbing which is light brown in colour and made from jute fibre, usually used in a 5 cm (2 in) width but can be obtained in other widths. It will often be found that the older upholstery will have 7.5 cm (3 in) width supporting the filling or springs.

The former type is the better webbing but, of course, is much more expensive than jute webbing. In each of the two types there are a number of varying qualities available. In refurbishing a good reproduction or genuine antique seat it is prudent to use the best quality webbing that can be afforded. Jute webbing, particularly the 5 cm (2 in) width, has a far more limited useful life than its black and white counterpart.

Webbing must be lightly tensioned when being applied to a seat frame. Unlike rubber webbing where the length is increased by stretching, with woven webbing it is only necessary to take away the slackness. A good method of testing the tension of the webbing is whilst using the tensioning tool to tap the surface of the webbing with the side of the hammer that is being used. In the initial stage where no tension has been given, the hammer when struck against the surface of the web will give a dull sound, but as pressure is applied to strain the webbing, it will give off a drumming sound. Once the hammer is bouncing nice and lively and the drumming sound appears, that is sufficient tension and the webbing can then be tacked. It is unwise to tack webbing loosely as the filling will sag with the webbing after a short term of use.

On no account overstretch the woven webbing as this will damage the webbing and the frame and in all probability it would cause the frame to twist from the flat so that it will 'rock' in the chair rebate and the joints will be damaged.

Figure 31 shows the sequence of applying webbing to a loose seat frame. 13 mm ($\frac{1}{2}$ in) tacks should be used, hammered

35. Using upholsterer's webbing tool

home straight with the heads flat (it is as well to practise this on an old piece of timber if you find it difficult). Should the tacks enter the timber at an angle, remove them and replace with a fresh tack. The webbing will be far stronger if this is done.

Do *not* cut off each strand individually before starting. It will be impossible to tension the short lengths, so work from the roll or length you have available, tacking the ends first, before tensioning and cutting off so that there is no waste. Two ends of the webbing can be used simultaneously. To overcome the difficulty of keeping the seat flat whilst tensioning the webbing, tack a piece of the old webbing over the seat rail on the opposite side to which you are straining the webbing, or around the two sides. Tack this webbing on to the worktop and remove it after the tensioning is completed. It is an advantage to work with the front rail of the seat frame furthest from you. Tack the webbing on the front rail working the centre web first and then the outer strands. Tension the webbing towards you. Should you be applying four strands of webbing on a carver chair seat or elbow chair seat, apply the two side webs first, then space the other two between.

The normal number of strands to use on the average small dining chair loose seat would be 3 × 2 strands, that is, three strands front to back with two running across the seat. A larger seat, i.e. elbow or carver chair seat, should have 3 × 3 for satisfactory suspension, or even 4 × 3 if extra large.

Strands of woven webbing should be interlaced alternately passing over or under the next web in addition to tensioning the strands so that each will help to support the remainder.

Follow the sequence as shown in figure 31.

1. Mark centres on front and back rails.
2. Make a $1\frac{1}{2}$ cm (5/8 in) fold at the end of the loose webbing.
3. Using 13 mm ($\frac{1}{2}$ in) tacks, tack the folded end of webbing down to the frame approximately about half the distance across the width of the front rail (this should be furthest from you). Put in five tacks in a staggered formation as shown – this method will assist in preventing the wood splitting.

Using the webbing stretcher or piece of wood as shown in figures 15a/b and figures 35 and 36, apply tension to the webbing

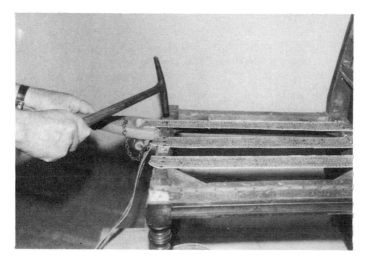

36. Tacking webbing after tensioning

with one hand. Hold the stretcher steady whilst hammering the tack through the webbing into the timber. Three tacks should be put in, one each side of the web close to the sides and one in the centre.

Interlacing of the webbing is done with the webs stretching side to side. These are also tacked folded on the first end and tacked single on the second. After tensioning and tacking, surplus webbing should be trimmed off leaving sufficient to make a further fold-over of $1\frac{1}{2}$ cm ($\frac{5}{8}$ in). After hammering down the fold-over, put in two further tacks which should be positioned to give the same staggered formation as at the other end, except three of the tacks which are under the fold. The webbing should now be drum tight.

Hessian base

A good quality hessian, minimum 12 oz quality, should now be laid over the webbing, making a fold-over of approximately 1.2 cm ($\frac{1}{2}$ in) along one edge. This should be tacked along the fold onto the front rail of the seat frame just beyond the folded ends of the webs so that these are covered. Using 13 mm ($\frac{1}{2}$ in) tacks approximately 4 cm ($1\frac{1}{2}$ in) apart, tack along the fold almost to each side rail.

Tension the hessian as tightly as possible with the fingers towards the opposite rail, closest to you. Tack on the single thickness of hessian using the same spacing. Start tensioning and tacking in the centre and work towards either side so the hessian is being strained towards the sides in addition to towards you. Tack single thickness down right or left side, strain the hessian and again tack single thickness to the opposite side. The weave of the hessian should appear straight and in line with the edge of the seat frame at this stage. Trim off surplus hessian leaving approximately 2 cm ($\frac{3}{4}$ in) to fold over and tack down as reinforcement to the hessian tacked below.

Bridling ties

The loose horsehair to be used will need to be held in position with twine ties (these were cut away when stripping the seat). Figure 37 shows positions and number of loops needed for the average seat. Twine is sewn into the base hessian using an upholsterer's spring

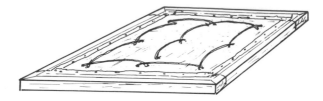

37. Twine bridle ties on seat

needle or a large semi-circular needle with an eye large enough to accept twine.

Two loops of twine should be sewn into the hessian on each side approximately 7.5 cm (3 in) away from the outer edges of the frame. The loops should be left just a little slack to allow filling to be tucked under. A good guide for this is to lay the palm of one hand on the hessian and allow the twine to drape loosely over the top of the hand. Loops should be formed with a running line only knotting the first and last stitches into the hessian, the remainder being free to move through the weave of the hessian as the filling is being tucked under the loops.

Horsehair filling
The original filling of horsehair may be re-used. Generally, a seat which has been upholstered many years ago will have been stuffed with good quality horsehair. Today, an equivalent quality would be very difficult to obtain and would be very expensive.

Should you decide to re-use the original filling, it must be 'teased' back to life. The horsehair from the original upholstery will be found to be tightly compacted into a matted mass. This can be 'opened' or 'teased' by painstakingly pulling the mass apart until it becomes a larger bulk of loose curly hair. Unfortunately this is a lengthy and very dusty operation (carding is usually done by machine). It is wise to wear a protective mask over the mouth and nostrils to prevent inhalation of dust. A method used many years ago was to have two bat-shaped pieces of wood with a mass of nails protruding, placing a wad of horsehair between and moving the bats back and forth, the hair slowly became untangled. This job is best done in the open air.

Figure 38 shows how horsehair is tucked under the bridling ties. The loose hair is picked up in a convenient handful and placed under the ties. Work around each side first, then complete the filling of the centre portion. There should be a slight doming towards the centre with the hair completely covering the hessian and timber around the edges (*not over the edge*).

38. Inserting filling under bridle ties

Undercovering
With filling satisfactorily placed without any lumpiness or unevenness, the undercover should be laid over the filling, temporary tacked and tacked off as described on pages 29 to 30 on an earlier example.

Fitting
At this stage it is prudent to fit the seat into the chair rebate trying a double thickness sample of the new covering fabric. Any adjustments required should be undertaken as detailed on pages 19 to 21.

Before the covering is applied, a minimum of two layers of skin wadding should be laid over the undercovered seat. This should be trimmed off at the top edges around the frame. It is vital *not* to allow the wadding to extend down the sides of the seat frame. Putting wadding over the surface of the undercover will prevent the spiky horsehair from working through the top covering. The skin of the wadding should be placed on the underside with the soft surface uppermost.

Covering

Fabric covering should be applied as described for the previous example on pages 21 to 23. Whilst covering is being temporary tacked into position and finally tacked, ensure that the underlying wadding is not disturbed. Should any work its way down the edges on any side, cut or pull the surplus away. Should any be left there, there will be added thickness on the covering at the edges and it will make the seat too bulky to fit the rebate of the chair. Bottoming fabrics should be applied as described on page 23.

Leather covering

Leather is a most satisfactory covering material to work with. It always looks good, has a pleasant odour and gives a chair an expensive and smart look.

Unfortunately leather suitable for upholstery covering is rather difficult to obtain in a small quantity sufficient for, say, 1 seat or even 4 seats.

Leather processors deal direct with upholstery manufacturers and supply leather in whole skins averaging about 4.47 to 4.65 sq. metres (48/50 sq. ft.) – a whole skin is very expensive. Occasionally half skins are available but even this quantity is far in excess of the amateur's requirement.

There is, however, a possibility that if you happen to reside in an area close to a leather processor or supplier of leather, you could buy a small offcut from a faulty skin at a reasonable price.

Leather, of course, is usually thicker than most woven fabric. Therefore, if leather is to be used to replace an original fabric, the seat frame will most likely need reducing slightly for a sliding fit into the rebate of the chair.

Particular care must be taken when pleating corners. It is as well to rasp or sand away rather more of the wood at the extreme corners to accommodate the extra thickness of the fold of the leather.

Modern leather, unlike leather on old chairs, is quite pliable and soft. It is, therefore, easy to work. Do not over-stretch the soft leather; ease the looseness out just as gently as fabric is worked. Whilst working, take care that the seat is not turned top face down on loose tacks over the worktop. Leather is easily scratched and this will ruin the appearance of the finished item.

Simulated leather

Most varieties of imitation leather, i.e. P.V.C., expanded vinyl and polyurethane-coated fabric, are relatively easy to purchase from a number of sources. If you are after that 'leather' appearance, there are a number of very good imitations available. These are a good deal cheaper than leather. As with fabric, two seats will be obtained from the full width of the cloth. The thickness too does not pose much of a problem because most varieties of this type of covering are no thicker than fabric; some are even thinner.

Re-tightening leather on old seats

Frequently an old chair which has had its loose seat covered with leather, will show a slight dip in the centre of the seat. Generally, the leather becomes loose and wrinkled at the point of the dip. This is unsightly and can be remedied.

Leather used in some of the earlier upholstery was often thicker and tougher than that available today, and was more difficult to work. To refurbish a seat in the condition described above, it is necessary to remove the leather covering carefully after taking off the bottoming fabric. The old leather may be a little brittle or have perished in places so great care is needed. Remove the wadding and the undercovering. Re-tease the hair or other filling to enliven the centre portion in particular. Replace or renew the undercovering. Replace the wadding or renew.

Handling the old leather carefully, temporary tack all round. It now needs tensioning to remove the ingrained looseness where the leather has been stretched in the centre.

Figure 39 shows how the leather can be stretched using 'molegrips' if it is impossible to remove the wrinkling by hand straining. The upholsterer will have a special tool for this operation, a pair of pliers with wide jaws but, of course, the reader will not

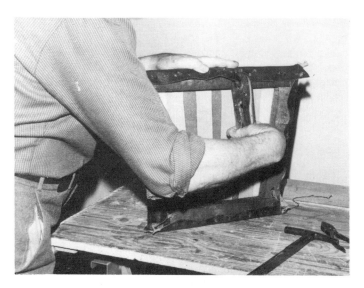

39. Tensioning leather using Molegrips

40. Altar kneeling stool with loose seat covered with
hand-embroidered covering

have access to this tool, so 'molegrips' are a substitute. When using the grips be extremely careful that the leather does not tear or split as old leather will have weakened over the years.

Figure 40 shows a altar kneeling stool with upholstered detachable seat with hand-embroidered covering.

FULLY-UPHOLSTERED DINING CHAIR SEATS

The term 'fully-uphostered chair seat' infers that the upholstery is fixed or tacked to the main chair seat frame, unlike the 'loose' seat which is upholstered as a separate unit away from the main frame.

Most dining chairs have a decorative finish of some kind, i.e. polish or a coating of some modern type of finish. This, of course, must not be damaged during the upholstering process so care must be exercised to that end.

A fully-upholstered fixed chair seat can be upholstered by the modern method using modern materials, i.e. latex or polyurethane foam, rubber webbing and some form of modern spring. The modern method of upholstery is much quicker than the traditional style of work.

Older chairs and antique chairs will have been upholstered using true traditional methods and materials such as horse or pig hair (often mixed), fibre covered in scrim and stitched with twine into a roll around the edges. Some seats may have coil springs inside, set on woven webbing. Other seats, although upholstered using traditional fillings, may have been upholstered in a less time consuming way by taking 'short-cuts' which are not apparent in the final appearance of the seat.

A number of examples and varying methods of upholstery of fixed chair seats using modern and traditional methods and materials are described and shown here. The first described is re-upholstery of a top-stuffed Victorian style chair seat. Many of these are still very much in evidence and are still used in many homes.

TOP-STUFFED VICTORIAN CHAIR SEATS

Many chair seats of this period were upholstered with coil springs but for this example we shall omit the springing process, introducing it at a later stage.

A stuffed seat, such as in figure 41 which we are dealing with in this section, invariably collapses or wears badly along the front edge of the seat as it gets older, frequently causing the covering to split or burst open exposing the inner upholstery.

41. A stuffed and stitched seat

Covering used during the Victorian period, and for some time later, on this type of chair seat frequently was 'Leathercloth'.

This was the first attempt to imitate the leather appearance so sought after in those days. Leather was too expensive for the average household – in fact, this was the forerunner of our modern P.V.C.

TOOLS
> Ripping chisel or old screwdriver
> Mallet or hammer
> Scissors, pincers or pliers

Stripping seat

With a top-stuffed seat normally there will be no 'bottoming' material to remove from under the chair seat. If any has been used it will be covering the webbing and tacked on the top of the seat frame.

If the original covering was leathercloth there will be decorative nails or studs around the rebate of the seat on all sides, perhaps with a decorative banding to cover the tacks holding the covering. Carefully remove the nails or studs and the banding if any, using a sharp screwdriver and pressing its blade into the base of the nail head to lever it out. Do not allow the tool to slip and score the polish. There often is difficulty with removing the domed antique nails especially if these have been 'close' nailed.

Remove covering, carefully stripping tacks out of the wood parallel with the polished rebate.

Remove wadding and undercovering. This will expose the hair or other filling which is referred to as the 'second' stuffing. This is put over the 'first' stuffing which may be fibre of some kind or dried seaweed (Alva) with a covering of scrim. The 'second' stuffing will be held in with twine loops which should be cut to release the top filling.

'First' stuffing scrim will be held down with small tacks hammered into a bevel on the extreme top edges of the seat frame. Remove these tacks carefully stripping them out sideways *with* the grain to avoid damage to the bevel; we shall need to re-use this later. Once the tacks are removed on the four sides, lift up the edges of the stitched seat and cut through the twine ties holding the mass to the base hessian. Hessian and webbing may now be removed leaving the virgin frame.

Materials

	1 SEAT	4 SEATS
Webbing	2.30m ($2\frac{1}{2}$ yds)	9.20 m (10 yds)
Hessian	46 cm × 46 cm (18 in × 18 in)	46 cm × 72 in width (18 in × 72 in)
		or 92 cm × 36 in width (36 in × 36 in)
Fibre	1 kg (2 lbs)	4 kg (8 lbs)
Upholsterer's scrim	60 cm × 60 cm (24 in × 24 in)	60 cm × 72 in width (24 in × 72 in)
(or loosely-woven hessian)		+ 60 cm × 60 cm (24 in × 24 in)
Hair	1/2 kg (1 lb)	2 kgs (4 lbs)
Calico	60 cm × 60 cm (24 in × 24 in)	60 cm × 72 in width (24 in × 72 in)
		+ 60 cm × 60 cm (24 in × 24 in)
Skin wadding	60 cm × 91 cm (24 in × 36 in)	2.50 m × 91 cm (3 yds × 36 in)
Covering	56 cm × 1/2 width (22 in × 24 in)	1.12 m × 48/50 in width
		($1\frac{1}{4}$ yds × 48/50 in width)
Bottoming (may be omitted)	46 cm × 46 cm (18 in × 18 in)	46 cm × 72 in width (18 in × 72 in width)
Trimming Gimp	1.75 m (2 yds)	$7\frac{1}{2}$ m (8 yds)

TOOLS

Upholsterer's hammer or light cabinet hammer
Scissors
Upholsterer's regulator
Upholsterer's spring needle or large semi-circular needle
   to take twine
20 cm or 25 cm (8 in or 10 in) upholsterer's straight
   needle
Webbing stretcher or substitute piece of wood
Wood rasp or coarse file

Reupholstery of seat

Before commencement of upholstery, check frame joints, particularly corner braces. Any loose joints should be tapped lightly apart; clean away surplus adhesive, apply fresh adhesive and cramp together using a sash cramp (*figure 33*) or using the handy device shown in figure 34 available in most D.I.Y. stores. Corner braces may need regluing or their screws tightened. Clean off any loose splinters from the bevel on top edge of seat rails to which the scrim was tacked. It is wise to increase the width of the bevel slightly using a wood rasp or very rough file but retain the existing angle of the bevel which should be approximately 45°.

Webbing

Use the best quality webbing available, preferably 5.0 cm (2 in) black and white herringbone striped webbing, or 5.0 cm (2 in) brown jute as a poorer quality alternative. For a normal 'top' stuffed seat 3×2 or 3×3 strands of webbing should be used. These should be tacked upon the *top* surface of the seat rails (*figure 4*). Work from centre placing first web folded with approximately 2 cm ($\frac{3}{4}$ in) fold and using five 13 mm ($\frac{1}{2}$ in) tacks. Webbing should be placed about half-way across width of rail. Do *not* cut webbing into short lengths before tacking. Work from the roll or the length available; short lengths cannot be tensioned sufficiently. Tension the centre web; ensure it is straight. Use the webbing stretcher or a substitute. Test tensioning with a light tap of the hammer; it should give a drumming sound if correct. Hammer three tacks into the single thickness web, one in the centre and the remaining two close to the outside edges of the web. Trim off surplus, leaving approximately 2 cm ($\frac{3}{4}$ in) for fold-over, this being tacked down with a further two tacks. Try to attain the staggered formation to avoid splitting the timber. Now apply the two outer webs using the two ends of your length of webbing; it is easier to gauge spacing this way. These should be tacked as the centre strand. All should be nicely spaced and should the seat be tapered towards the rear of the frame, webbing should follow that line. Now apply webbing side to side, not forgetting to interlace alternately, as if weaving. Strands side to side should be tensioned and tacked as were strands back to front. Do not omit tacking the fold-over of the ends.

Hessian

Hessian of good quality should be used, i.e. a minimum quality of 366 gms per sq m (12 oz) (mostly referred to as 12 oz hessian). A fold of approximately 12 mm ($\frac{1}{2}$ in) should be made along one side. Should the piece of hessian have a selvedge along one side, make the fold along the selvedge edge. Tack the fold along the length of the back, over the webbing and slightly beyond to completely cover folds of the webs, spacing the 13 mm ($\frac{1}{2}$ in) tacks approximately 3.5 cm ($1\frac{1}{2}$ in). Then tension the hessian towards you as tightly as possible with the hand. Tack single thickness starting at the centre, then work towards each corner, tensioning towards the corner as each successive tack is put in. Tack singly along one side, then tension across to the other and tack, three sides being tacked on the single hessian; trim away surplus hessian leaving sufficient to form a fold of approximately 1.5 cm ($\frac{3}{4}$ in). The fold is tacked down on the three sides to reinforce the single thickness tacking below.

Bridling ties

Loops of twine are threaded into the base hessian using the upholsterer's spring needle or the large semi-circular needle. Two loops are adequate around the sides – these should run parallel with the outside line of the seat but approximately 7.5 cm (3 in) in from the edge. Two loops are also needed down the centre front to back (*figure 42*). Loops should be slack with loose twine to allow filling to be inserted beneath. Lay the hand, slightly cupped, on the surface of the hessian and allow the twine to lie over the back of the hand; this will be a guide to the amount of slackness needed.

42. 'Bridle' ties sewn into base hessian

Applying filling

Previously, the list of materials specified quantities of fibre and hair separately. Often when an old chair is stripped, it is found to contain horsehair both in its 'first' and 'second' stuffing. Using fibre in the 'first' stuffing of a seat is a method of economy adopted in more recent times because of the shortage and therefore high price of horsehair. If you wish, you can use horsehair for both 'first' and 'second' stuffing.

Many Victorian chair seats and other items of upholstery were frequently stuffed using 'Alva marino' – a dried seaweed. Should you have stripped this out from your chair seat, it should be discarded and fresh filling obtained. Also with the dried seaweed, as a 'second' stuffing, cotton 'flock' was used – unfortunately this should also be discarded. Horse or pig hair mixture is probably the only re-usable filling, provided it is well 'teased' and opened. This can be accomplished manually by pulling the hair apart. It is prudent to wear a protective mask and do the job in the open air, out-of-doors.

To re-use the original filling, the stitched seat filling, with the covering of scrim which was removed, must be taken apart by cutting through the two or three rows of close twine stitching. This is best done with a sharp pointed knife such as a 'Stanley' trimming knife. The old scrim should be discarded when the hair has been released.

Figure 38 shows how the hair or fibre is placed under the twine ties. Thickness of filling to be applied is dependent upon the height of the original seat and its stitching. This should have been noted earlier. The filling needs to be packed under the bridle ties around the edge quite densely but evenly without any lumpiness, working around all the sides first and then packing in the centre. After the completed filling operation the mass of filling should look quite flat at this stage; not piled up high in the centre of the seat.

Covering with upholsterer's scrim (or loosely-woven hessian)
Scrim should be cut roughly to size remembering a larger measurement is needed to work with than the measurement tight across; it must be applied very loosely over the filling. Also it must be temporary tacked on so that the weave is absolutely straight. Centres should be marked on front and back seat rails; also mark centres of scrim on front and back edges so they may be aligned.

Temporary tack scrim with tacks only half home on *face* of back rail ensuring the tacks are in the rebated edge, *not* in the polished edge should there be one. Smooth the scrim lightly over the filling towards and over the front temporary tacking again on the plain bare wood. Five tacks will be sufficient on each side at this stage. Use the largest tacks that you have available for this operation as small-headed tacks will tend to allow the scrim to pull away from the fixing points.

With the scrim reasonably tidy and straight but in its temporary tacked position, mark positions (with the point of the needle) where the twine stuffing ties will be passed through (*figure 41*). Needle and twine should pass *right through* the scrim, filling and base hessian, being pulled free on the underside of the seat. Re-enter with the needle and twine into the base hessian a few threads along and pass the needle and twine back through and out of the surface of the scrim again. Repeat this process for as many ties as are marked in the scrim. Twine should be free running, only knotting at the first tie to hold the twine in that position and the last position, this being knotted *after* the twine has been eased tightly along its length through each position so that it sinks into the surface of the scrim and filling.

Probably the most difficult part of the operation now follows – that of tacking the scrim down on to the bevelled top edges of the seat rails. The amount of scrim and filling needs to be gauged by trial and error to attain the desired height of finished stitched edge. Trim off surplus scrim if there appears to be an excessive amount. Ensure that the filling is firm along the edges. Remove the centre temporary tack on the front seat rail (this should have been placed on the face of the rail), fold the edge of the scrim *under* and tuck it under the filling. Holding the scrim in position with one hand, insert a tack into the scrim so that it is on the bevelled edge and hammer home. 10 mm ($\frac{3}{8}$ in) tacks should be used for this. Tacks should be quite close together, approximately 1 cm ($\frac{1}{2}$ in) apart.

After putting in five or six tacks along the bevel, test to see if the allowance of scrim is correct for the height intended for the edge of the seat. It is possible at this stage to use the fingers to pinch the scrim together (later on, the stitching will have this effect); the height will then be apparent. Possibly the initial tacking of the scrim may be too high or too low and should it not be satisfactory at this stage, it is easily remedied. With the initial tacks holding the scrim in its correct position, continue tacking along the full length of front edge. It is very important to ensure the scrim is tacked straight, i.e. follow the same line of thread weave along the complete length, that is, if the edge is a straight rail. Should there be a curve, the tacking of scrim will need to be adjusted to allow for the shape. Tacking along the back rail should be undertaken next and then the two sides; again these may be curved so adjustment in tacking the scrim may have to be made. Tack all four sides before any stitching is undertaken.

Stitching of edges

Stitching of edges is undertaken using a 20 cm or 25 cm (8 in or 10 in) length 'fine' or 'bayonet' point (triangular pointed end) needle and a good quality thin flax twine. Unfortunately, there is no substitute for an upholsterer's straight needle but they are available at some D.I.Y. stores which sell upholstery sundries, as is a 'Regulator' needle. Two or three rows of stitching may be needed dependent upon the final height of the top edge of the seat. A height of up to 3.5 cm ($1\frac{1}{2}$ in) from the bevel should require two rows of stitching, i.e. 1 row of 'blind' stitching and 1 row of 'fine' top stitching. Above that height three rows are recommended, i.e. one row of 'blind' stitching, one row of 'roll' stitching and one row of 'fine' top stitching.

The object of the row of 'blind' stitching is to form loops within the scrim to gather filling and compact it around the edges to be stitched. As the name implies, it is *not* visible on the top surface of the scrim.

Stitching is normally undertaken working from left to right. Insert a length of twine approximately 1.25 m (50 in) into the eye of the needle. Starting from the left-hand corner of the seat adjacent to the left-hand leg, insert the needle point into the scrim approximately 4 cm ($1\frac{1}{2}$ in) from the leg and 1.2 cm ($\frac{1}{2}$ in) up from the tacked edge of the scrim.

Push needle at an angle of about 45° into scrim edge face (*figure 43*). Allow the point of the needle to emerge through the top surface of the seat only so far as to draw the twine into the filling interior (without completely withdrawing it). As the needle is

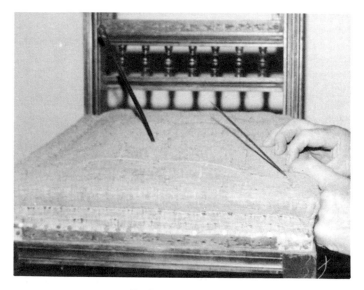

43. Stitching 'roll stitch'

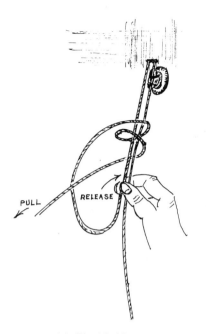

44. The 'slip' knot

pushed back, gently ease it towards the right about 15° so the *point* emerges about 12 mm ($\frac{1}{2}$ in) to the *left* of the entry point. Pull the needle completely through and make a slip knot (*figure 44*) at the point of entry and exit. Ease this knot tight. If done correctly there should be a slight movement of the filling forward, compacting it ready for the following row of stitching. Repeat this for the second stitch but instead of forming a slip knot, as the point of the needle emerges from the face of the scrim, turn the length of twine hanging to the *left* of the needle twice anti-clockwise around the needle. This will form a knot as the twine is eased tight. After twisting the twine around the needle twice, gently but firmly ease the twine tight so that the filling is felt to move slightly forward. Continue the 'blind' stitch on the remainder of all the edges.

Should the twine become too short to continue stitching, say 25 cm (10 in) remaining, knot off the end to prevent the twine slipping back and re-start with a fresh length starting with a 'slip' knot again as at the commencement of the row.

Assuming three rows of stitching will be needed, the next two rows will appear on the surface of the scrim (unlike the 'blind' stitch). Starting again at the back left-hand leg with approximately the same length of twine as before, with the needle and twine handy, pinch the scrim and filling with two fingers to form a roll approximately 2.5 cm to 3.0 cm (1 in to $1\frac{1}{4}$ in) thick. This will enable judgement to be made as to where to insert the needle to make a roll of a suitable size (*figure 43*). Having established the positions for inserting the needle, the needle and twine may be pushed through the scrim approximately 2 cm ($\frac{3}{4}$ in) from the back leg taking the needle and twine completely through and threading back again *towards* the back leg making a stitch length of about 10 mm ($\frac{3}{8}$ in). There should be a continuous line of stitches with no gaps as the needle travels along, always taking the needle *back* to make each stitch and turning the twine anti-clockwise around the needle as before. After each stitch is formed, the twine should be pulled tight to cause the twine stitch to sink into the scrim and filling to give a *firm* stitch. Continue to stitch the roll on all four sides. The roll should be the size of a rather thick thumb. Left-handed workers should work the reverse direction, i.e. right to left.

The final stitch, a 'fine' top stitch is a repeat of the 'roll' stitch but should have rather less scrim and filling taken up between the needle entry and exit points to create a small rather firm, smooth and sharp edge to give the covering a good foundation. Throughout the stitching process the height of the edge stitching should be checked constantly to ensure it is as intended and is of an equal height on all sides (*figure 41*).

With the stitching completed, twine bridle ties should be sewn into the surface of the scrim using a 'spring' needle or large circular needle in the same fashion as with the base hessian. Bridle ties on the surface of the scrim should be slightly tighter than the earlier ties to accommodate less filling.

The 'second' or 'top' stuffing of hair should be evenly placed under the ties using the outer ties first. Tuck under just sufficient filling to fill the shallow hollow or channel made by the stitching, then filling the centre ties with the filling gently domed to the centre. Filling should be evenly placed and free of any uneven-ness or lumps.

Undercovering and covering

Over the second layer of filling should be placed an undercover of lining, calico or similar material cut roughly to size with enough surplus for handling purposes. This should be tacked into position using 13 mm ($\frac{1}{2}$ in) tacks. Make sure that the threads are straight and that temporary tacks are *not* hammered into the polished face of the seat rails.

45. Cutting covering at back leg 'stile'

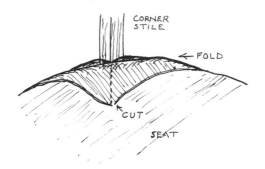

46. Cutting covering at back leg 'stile'

Figures 45 and 46 show how the undercover and top covering is cut at the corners to accommodate the back legs. To cut corners around arm stiles, cut towards the centre of the arm member and v-cut out towards the outer edges. After the diagonal cut is made towards the back leg, surplus material is tucked down between the scrim and filling and the back leg. The material can be eased down with a regulator or any flat strong device. Undercovering should be tacked home finally using 10 mm ($\frac{3}{8}$ in) tacks aiming at approximately half-way between the top of the seat rail where the scrim is fixed and the polished rebate edge. Take care not to hit the polished rebate with the hammer. Whilst tacking, smooth the undercover fabric with the palm of the hand to work the slackness over the stitched edge and finally pull out slackness with the fingers and tack off. Front corners should be pleated on front edge if corners are square, using two 'fan' pleats if the corner has a radius (*figure 47*).

A minimum of two layers of skin wadding or suitable thickness of other wadding should be laid between the undercovering and top covering. It should be laid smoothly without wrinkles. Take the wadding over the sides, front and back edges approximately half-way down each edge between the top and tacking position at rebate or the chair bottom edge. Covering should be placed carefully so as not to disturb the wadding, using 10 mm ($\frac{3}{8}$ in) tacks for tacking off the covering at the rebate or under chair frame.

Should the covering have a central pattern or motif, ensure that it is arranged on the seat to maximum effect. A central pattern should be placed slightly forward of centre, i.e. 2 cm ($\frac{3}{4}$ in).

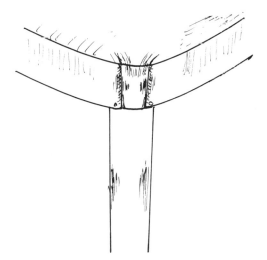

47. 'Fan' pleating at radius corner

Placing dead centre tends to give the appearance of not being central when viewed from the normal viewing position. Temporary tack top covering adequately; double check before attempting to tack finally. When you are working to a rebate, ensure that the tacks are placed to allow the trimming gimp to cover them. Gimp is applied with an adhesive (not the contact type) and applied with a narrow spatula thinly along the back surface. Press the gimp firmly along the covering in the appropriate position in lengths of approximately 15 cm to 20 cm (6 in to 8 in) at a time. Hold the gimp in position with temporary tacks which will be removed when the adhesive has set (*figure 48*).

Should the covering be plastic-coated or leather, woven gimp is unsuitable as a finish. Banding and covered studs or oxidised or brass decorative nails should be used (*figure 5*). Simulated leather-type covering or leather covering should be tacked off using 'gimp' pins. Gimp pins are very fine tacks with small heads, generally supplied black japanned, but available in many colours to suit the colour of the covering being used. It is easier to hide these smaller gimp pins with the decorative nails.

Bottoming is not normally applied to a 'top' stuffed seat such as this example.

48. Applying adhesive to gimp trimming

Using springs

Many examples of Victorian upholstered small chair seats are
sprung using coil springs of 10 cm/12.5 cm (4/5 in) height. These
are an alternative to the 'top' stuffed seat in the previous example.

It is fairly common when refurbishing a sprung seat to find
the coil springs to be 'crippled', i.e. when standing free, the coils
may be deformed and the spring bent. In this condition a spring is
unsuitable for re-use. Springs should be re-used only if, when
standing free, they stand erect and when pressed down with the
hand do not tilt over. Should some springs be found to be 'crippled', it is wise to renew all. Strength of the springs, i.e. thickness of

the spring wire, should be 10 S.W.G. or perhaps a stronger 9 S.W.G. (S.W.G. = standard wire gauge).

Stripping sprung seat

A bottoming cover would normally be tacked on the underside of the sprung seat. On removal of the bottoming you will find webbing tacked on the base of the seat frame, unlike the 'top' stuffed example which had webbing tacked on the top surface.

When stripping a sprung seat, work methodically removing the upholstery from the top, working from the covering down to the springing. Then turn the seat over, cut the twine holding springs to the webbing and then remove the webbing.

The number of springs used in a sprung seat may vary. Some seats have five springs only, others seven, and others eight or nine springs. Figures 49 and 50 show examples of how the top coils of the springs are lashed to prevent lateral movement.

49. Dining chair seat with five springs

50. Dining chair seat with eight springs

Webbing and sewing in springs

Ample good quality, preferably black and white linen webbing should be used, i.e. 3 × 3 strands or 4 × 3 strands, interlaced and tacked with 13 mm ($\frac{1}{2}$ in) tacks to give adequate support for the springing. Webbing should be well tensioned using webbing stretcher or substitute as in earlier examples.

The base of the springs should be sewn to the webbing from the underside of the webbing using 3 or 4 ties, each tie knotted. When passing the straight, large semi-circular or upholsterer's spring needle (any of these may be used) through the webbing and returning through the web on the other side of the wire, twist twine once around the needle – this will form a knot if pulled tightly (*figure 51*).

70

51. Seat springs sewn to base webbing

Tops of springs should be 'lashed' or tied (*figures 49 and 50*) either diagonally or side to side and back to front depending upon the number of springs. The cords are tacked on the top surface of seat rails.

Outer springs should be lashed with a slight tilt from the centre towards the outer rails.

With springs lashed securely, a good quality hessian should be tacked over. It should be single thickness on the upper surface of the seat rails on all sides, approximately in the centre of the rail. After trimming, a fold-over is made with further tacking using 13 mm ($\frac{1}{2}$ in) tacks as reinforcement. Hessian over the springs should be taut with no slackness. Do not reduce the height of springs by straining the hessian too tightly.

Top coil of each spring should now be sewn to the hessian using twine and a large semi-circular or spring needle, making either three or four ties through the hessian to lock the coil firmly to the hessian. As the needle is passed through the hessian to catch the spring wire and eased out again on the other side of the wire, turn the loose end of twine once around the needle to form a knot at each position (*figure 52*).

52. Top coils of springs sewn to hessian, bridle ties also in position

At this stage bridle ties should be sewn into the hessian to hold the filling as we did for the base hessian of the 'top' stuffed seat in the previous example. Filling of the sprung seat should not be *over* domed. Its appearance should be reasonably flat as the 'top' stuffed style.

The following processes are as explained in the example on pages 59–67.

Back of chair

Back panel of chair as shown may be upholstered with a roll sewn around each side as in figure 53 giving a deep upholstered finish. Alternatively, the back may be 'pin' stuffed as shown in Fig. 79 **a** and **b**.

53. Upholstery of chair back

TACK-ROLL EDGE SEAT

The stuffing and stitching process explained in the previous section is a trying and difficult operation for many. However, there is a simpler process which is often adopted and which has a similar finished appearance to stitching an edge. This is frequently done professionally. One can look upon the tack-roll method as a short cut.

The object of forming a tack-roll around the edges of the seat is to make a reasonably soft edge with a certain amount of depth. This method is less time consuming than stitching with needle and twine. A tack-roll can be used on a 'top' stuffed seat and one with springs.

Figure 54 shows the commencement of the process, tacking a strip of hessian approximately 9 cm ($3\frac{1}{2}$ in) wide on a bevel made by rasping along the extreme top corner edge of the seat rail. A fold is made in the hessian before tacking on the bevel. Some form of filling is laid along the edge; the hessian is then wrapped over the filling and tucked under on the inner side, compressing the filling until a suitable size roll is made and a satisfactory firmness is achieved. A suitable thickness for a normal tack-roll would be finger or thumb thickness. With the hessian rolled tightly around the filling, it should be tacked on the top edge of the rail as shown in figure 54. 13 mm ($\frac{1}{2}$ in) tacks are most suitable for this process being spaced approximately 13 mm ($\frac{1}{2}$ in). The object of this exercise is, of course, to make a *smooth* edge line.

54. Making a 'tack-roll'

After making the tack-roll, continue upholstering as follows: Place the filling behind the roll fairly firmly to fill up the channel behind the roll. Then fill in the rest of the seat and cover this in calico or lining, follow with wadding and covering as in previous instructions.

Foam interior chair seat

MATERIALS

      Webbing, woven 2.5 m (3 yds), rubber 1.75 m (2 yds)

      Foam, 6 cm/7.5 cm ($2\frac{1}{2}$ in/3 in) thickness, firm density,

      46 cm × 46 cm (18 in × 18 in)

      Calico or linen, 60 cm × 60 cm (24 in × 24 in)

      Covering, 60 cm × 60 cm (24 in × 24 in)

      Adhesive

      13 mm ($\frac{1}{2}$ in) tacks (or staples)

    The use of latex or polyurethane foam as a filling for re-upholstering a dining chair will, no doubt, be preferred by many because it is simple to use and because there are no problems with availability of supplies. Figure 48 shows a dining chair seat upholstered in such a manner.

    After stripping off all old upholstery, tack 3 × 3 strands of linen or jute woven webbing, or 3 × 2 strands of resilient rubber webbing.

Upholstering

Webbing should be tacked onto the top surface of seat frame rails using 13 mm ($\frac{1}{2}$ in) tacks. Woven webbing needs to be tensioned with the webbing stretcher or a substitute. Rubber webbing can be hand-tensioned at approximately $7\frac{1}{2}\%$ to 10% stretch. The method used for checking this tension is explained on pages 32–33.

    Next, mark foam around the sides of the seat (*figure 55*). 6 cm or 7.5 cm ($2\frac{1}{2}$ in or 3 in) foam may be used; cut the foam 6 mm ($\frac{1}{4}$ in) oversize on all sides (*figure 56*). A strip of soft material, such as calico or lining, should be stuck along the face edges on all sides. This will act as a tacking strip to hold foam in position; this should be tacked on face sides of rails (*figures 57 and 58*).

    With foam fixed in position, it is advisable to trim off as evenly as possible the sharp corner edge on all sides to give a slight radius (*figure 58*).

    An undercovering should be placed over the foam, such as lining or calico, before the main covering.

    Undercovering and covering should be cut around the back leg as shown in figures 45 and 46. After cutting the surplus

55. Marking foam around sides of seat

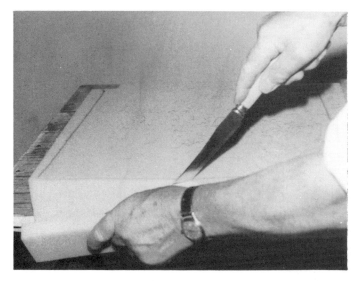

56. Cutting seat foam

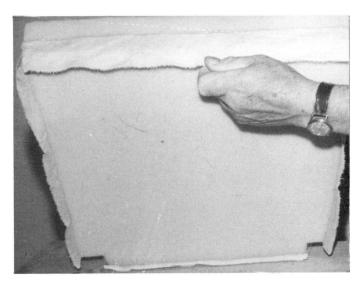

57. Calico flanges stuck around bottom edges of seat foam

58. Top edge trimmed off seat foam

material, each side of the diagonal cut should be smoothed and tucked down between the foam and back leg using a flat instrument.

It is not advisable to use sheet wadding undercovering on a foam seat as such wadding tends to split and tear with the deflection of the foam.

Top covering should be laid, centred, over the foamed seat, temporary tacked and finally tacked home. Should there be a rebate with polished face around the seat, the covering should be tacked slightly above the edge of the rebate, finishing with decorative gimp or braid or, if using simulated leather covering, finish with oxidised upholstery nails.

Seat squabs and kneeling hassocks

Seat squab cushions are used as much with contemporary upholstery as they were in the past when most seating was made of solid timber. Earlier, seat squab cushions were generally filled with lambswool or curled horsehair; these commodities were both freely available at that time.

The modern equivalent of this type of upholstery padding is Latex foam (rubber) or polyurethane foam (plastic); both these materials are easier and faster to work with. Of these two modern fillings Latex foam is the more resilient and lasting but is somewhat more expensive than the polyurethane foam, and in some areas is more difficult to obtain.

Sheet Latex foam generally can be supplied in 12 mm ($\frac{1}{2}$ in) and 25 mm (1 in) thickness sheets or in the softer 'pincore' form, for use in making cushions, etc. this can be purchased in thicknesses up to 10 cm (4 in). Pincore latex foam has small holes running through the thickness at intervals over its complete surface. In most cases the supplier will cut pincore foam to the customer's template size.

Polyurethane foam is probably more readily available to the amateur upholsterer; it is often found in D.I.Y. stores and in market places. Thicknesses vary from 12 mm ($\frac{1}{2}$ in) through to 10 cm (4 in) and foam is supplied in different densities (firmness). It is very important to use the density of foam most suitable for the task being undertaken; some grades of foam are very soft and may be totally unsuitable for certain projects. It is recommended that foam be examined and tested before purchase.

Yet another type of plastic foam is available which is much denser and has less resilience than the normal polyurethane. This is known as re-constituted foam or, more commonly, as 'chip' foam. This is readily recognisable from its distinctive, colourful look. It is made from granules or chips of various colours moulded together in sheet form. It has a rather coarser feel to it than ordinary polyurethane foam. This type of firmer foam is useful for work on items such as firm kneeling hassocks or foot cushions or even seat squabs for dining chairs, etc. Figure 59 shows a church kneeling hassock with a reconstituted foam interior, 7.5 cm (3 in) depth with a hand-embroidered covering.

59. Church kneeling hassock

In case you plan to upholster more than one of these seat squabs or kneeling hassocks, this foam is available in sheet form and, like other foams, can easily be cut with a broad-bladed sharp knife. Alternatively, the suppliers will no doubt cut the foam to a specified size.

It is advisable to undercover the foam with linen to make a permanent jacket before fitting an embroidered or other covering over. This will allow the covering greater freedom of movement than over the foam surface. The undercover needs to be wrapped around the foam with only the edges and corners being lightly hand-sewn.

The covering in the example shown in figure 59 has the embroidery wrapped over the top surface and sides with a black linen base sewn around the base edges; corners are slip-stitched after being pinned together.

The use of ordinary polyurethane for kneeling hassocks is not to be recommended due to 'bottoming' of the foam, that is, being easily compressed to the floor with the concentrated weight on a small area, such as that of a person kneeling on it.

In some churches it is still possible to come across very old kneeling hassocks stuffed with good quality curled horsehair contained in a canvas case with stitching around the sides. These may be remade reusing the original filling after the hair has been 'carded' or 'teased' to open the curled strands of hair to revitalise the filling.

CHAIR SEAT SQUAB CUSHION

MATERIALS

Filling, 1 kg ($2\frac{1}{4}$ lbs) approximately (depends upon size)
Hessian, 70 cm ($\frac{3}{4}$ yd) full width
Wadding, 1.40 m ($1\frac{1}{2}$ yds)
Covering, 0.75 m ($\frac{3}{4}$ yd)
Flax twine

TOOLS

Upholsterer's straight needle 20 cm (8 in) length
Upholsterer's skewers or long pins
Sewing machine

Making up

Figure 60 shows the stuffed hessian interior case for a 4 cm ($1\frac{1}{2}$ in) deep seat squab cushion filled with curled horsehair in the process of being stitched around the edges with the upholsterer's needle and twine and using a 'mattress' stitch. This type of stitching forms a small visible stitch on the face of the border with loops of twine in the interior of the squab. The stitch should be

60. Interior stuffed canvas for seat squab cushion

a continuous running line, as every two or three stitches are inserted, the last should be eased tight to allow the loops within to draw filling towards the edge, creating a more compact border.

The initial stage in making this seat squab cushion is to cut an actual finished size template (pattern) to the extreme edges of the seat where the squab is to fit, following shaped or curved lines if any. A second, larger template should now be made for cutting the hessian case, working with the initial template laid over the top. The second template should have an allowance all round of 12 mm ($\frac{1}{2}$ in) for machine seaming plus an allowance for the slight contours on the surface formed by the interior filling. This allowance should be an extra 2.5 cm (1 in) for each 30 cm (12 in) of the size of the template, i.e. if the actual finished size of the squab cushion is 46 cm (18 in) across, the extra allowance on the cutting template in addition to seaming allowance should be 4 cm ($1\frac{1}{2}$ in) – thus the actual size to be cut across would be 46 cm + 2.4 cm seaming + 4 cm filling allowance (18 in + 1 in + $1\frac{1}{2}$ in) = 52.4 cm ($20\frac{1}{2}$ in).

The larger template should be laid over hessian, folded double, for top and bottom panels. Cut neatly around the template keeping the weave straight and square. The border of the hessian case should have a finished width of 4 cm ($1\frac{1}{2}$ in) and should be cut 6 cm ($2\frac{1}{2}$ in) wide. This should be machined around the top panel and front and the two sides of the base panel leaving the bottom back open for filling purposes. After the normal seam has been made, this should then be 'edge' stitched to give a firmer line to the edges of the squab case.

Filling case

The filling should be teased or opened well and packed firmly into the hessian case, working across the front, then progressing down each side working to the centre. It is an aid to the filling process if the case is held down on the worktop with a temporary tack at each corner stretching the case taut. After filling, the remaining side should be sewn up by hand-stitching.

The filled squab case should be kept as flat as possible – to this end it is an advantage to place a board with a weight on it to be moved across the surface as the filling progresses forward.

61. Ruched seat squab cushion in chair with caned seat and back

Twine ties should now be passed through the hessian and filling at intervals in a number of positions (*figure 60*) tying each off separately. This should give a quilted effect.

Covering
Covering should be cut using the initial template but adding 1 cm ($\frac{3}{8}$ in) for seaming of covering on all sides. Again, the bottom back seam should be left unsewn to allow entry of the inner case.

The seams on the covering can be trimmed with ruche or piping ((*figure 61*). Ruche is sewn into the seam using the flange of ruche tightly woven. Piping should be cut on the bias at 45° from the straight weave (*figure 62*); it should be cut minimum 4 cm ($1\frac{1}{2}$ in) wide. After making up the piping, trim the flanges to an equal width to that of the seam allowance of the covering. Ruche and piping should be sewn to the top and bottom panels, and then borders should be machined in position.

Figure 63 shows a 'feather' edge squab cushion for a timber seat dining/kitchen chair. This has a foam interior using latex sheet 12 mm ($\frac{1}{2}$ in) deep. 'Reconstituted' foam is frequently used for the interior of these squab cushions.

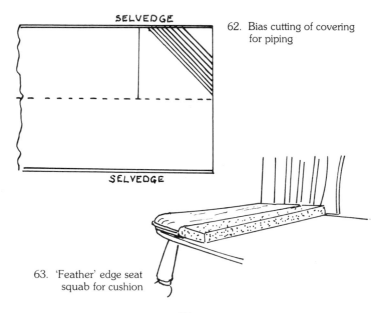

SELVEDGE

62. Bias cutting of covering for piping

SELVEDGE

63. 'Feather' edge seat squab for cushion

Filled pouffes and box pouffes

Today, pouffes are made in many forms and also in a variety of ways. The original floor pouffes were generally circular with some form of decorative pattern upon the circular top panel. These were filled with some form of economical loose filling. Very rarely were they stuffed with curled horsehair because of the amount of filling material required.

A typical inexpensive present-day production supplied by most furniture stores and in most homes is a type of floor pouffe with a covering of some type of plastic-coated material filled with 'wood wool', that is, fine strands of wood fibre similar to that used in packing 'fragile' items for transport to prevent breakage. The 'wood wool' is quite inexpensive but ideally suited for this purpose. It is frequently available, often at no charge, from stores dealing in good class chinaware and pottery. In fact, they are sometimes even pleased to have it removed from their premises.

Filling

When using wood fibre as a filling for a pouffe, the strands must be packed very firmly together into the inner case. Packing this type of filling loosely will allow the wood fibre to move and flex, resulting in a mass of short length fibres which lose filling power and reduce the size of the interior.

To make this kind of pouffe in either square or circular form, it is advisable firstly to machine a hessian or some other strong fabric case to the shape required, leaving part of the base at one side edge open to insert filling. This edge can be sewn by hand

64. Circular and square stuffed pouffes

after filling. The outer covering case can then easily be cut and fitted as one would a loose cover. Should the pouffe covering be made of soft, woven fabric, the base panel should be of P.V.C. This will give the pouffe better sliding qualities and prevent the kind of wear a soft material would get. The covering should be machined with the top panel and sides sewn together with either ruche or piping as trimming and the base sewn around after the covering is in position.

Circular pouffes

The top panel of a circular pouffe should be marked out as a perfect circle using twine to attain the circle (*figure 65*). When

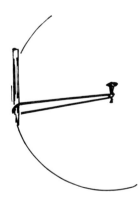

65. Marking a circle using twine

machining the side border to a circular top panel, it is very difficult to avoid distorting the circular shape especially in the sections where the threads are on a bias. To assist with this operation it is advisable, before attempting to machine the top border, to sew the perimeter of the circle with tacking stitches to a sheet of stout paper which has had the same circle size drawn upon it. This will enable the circular top panel to be worked without any distortion, the paper being torn away after machining. Some form of decorative trimming will be needed around the edge; either ruching or piping is suitable. It is particularly important when making up the piping for a circular item such as this, to ensure that fabric for piping is cut at 45° bias; cutting strips for piping straight across or along the length of the fabric will result in a puckered line or circle. Ruching should be eased in loosely whilst machining around the top of the pouffe. The side border should then be sewn on top of the ruche flange.

A length of decorative cord will be needed to match the ruche to pull in the centre using a decorative knot at the join of ends. It is most economical to have two joins in the side border from top to base (*figure 64*).

UPHOLSTERED BOX POUFFES

Figures 66 and 67 show an example of a simple but sturdy box pouffe covered in soft fabric with padded sides, upholstered lid and lined interior.

Figure 68 shows construction of the main frame and hardboard panels for exterior and interior. The frame is made fairly simply from timber of 3 cm × 4 cm ($1\frac{1}{8}$ in × $1\frac{1}{2}$ in) section hardwood.

Figure 69 shows a larger box pouffe constructed from chipboard, with making-up diagram. This may be covered in soft fabric or expanded vinyl plastic-coated fabric. The lid for this box pouffe may be upholstered plain with a wrap-over finish and may be 'float' buttoned or finished with deep diamond pleated buttoning.

Instructions are given for each of these types of lid upholstery.

66. Covered box pouffe

67. Lined interior of box pouffe

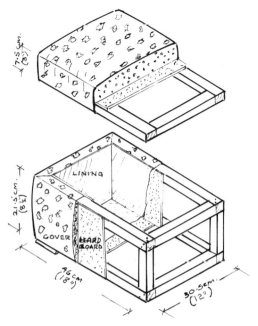

68. Construction of box pouffe

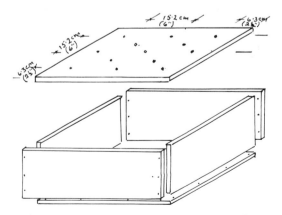

69. Construction of box pouffe using chipboard

89

Pouffe example (*Figure 66*)

Size 46 cm × 30.5 cm × 30.5 cm high (18 in × 12 in × 12 in high).

MATERIALS

Timber	6 pieces 46 cm (18 in length)
	6 pieces 23 cm (9 in length)
	4 pieces 13 cm (5 in length)
Hardboard	2 pieces 46 cm × 30.5 cm (18 in × 12 in)
	2 pieces 40.5 cm × 20.5 cm (16 in × 8 in)
	2 pieces 21.5 cm × 20.5 cm ($8\frac{1}{2}$ in × 8 in)
Foam	30.5 cm × 46 cm × 4 cm
	(12 in × 18 in × $1\frac{1}{2}$ in thick)
Covering	0.90 m (1 yd)
Fibre fill	1 m (1 yd) or wadding 2.75 m (3 yds)
Lining	0.75 m ($\frac{3}{4}$ yd)

13 mm ($\frac{1}{2}$ in) brads
13 mm ($\frac{1}{2}$ in) or 10 mm ($\frac{3}{8}$ in) tacks (or staples)
1 pair of brass hinges 4 cm ($1\frac{1}{2}$ in) and screws

Construction

The timber frame should be well glued and screwed, with the hardboard pieces cut to fit flush to appropriate edges of main frame.

Using 13 mm ($\frac{1}{2}$ in) brads, hardboard should be nailed to *outside* front and back faces and the two ends; do not nail the inner pieces or fit the lid at this stage (*figure 68*).

Upholstering

Cut the covering as shown in figure 70a.

Tack (or staple) covering along inside of the top edges approximately 13 mm ($\frac{1}{2}$ in) down from top edge. Tack so that covering face will be on the outside, on four sides.

With the four pieces tacked around the inside edges, take the covering down the outsides of the box but only put a few temporary tacks in around the outside bottom rails to prevent the covering from flapping about whilst attempting the next stage.

With the frame lying upon its side 'back-tack' (*figure 71*) the interior lining on one side fractionally down from top edge; tacks should be spaced about 4 cm ($1\frac{1}{2}$ in) apart. Then lay one of the

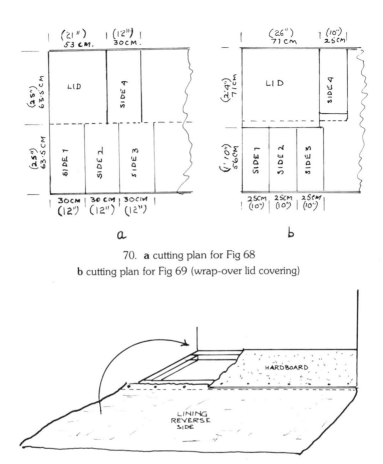

70. **a** cutting plan for Fig 68
b cutting plan for Fig 69 (wrap-over lid covering)

71. 'Back' tacking interior lining

long inner pieces of hardboard flush with the top edge over the tacked lining and nail down with brads; it should also be flush with the bottom rail. Lining should now be taken down and tacked along the *underside* of the base so that the inner hardboard is completely covered with no tacks visible on the interior face.

Treat the opposite long side in the same manner. Lining at ends may be tacked to corner posts. Do the same with the shorter ends. At corners, fold lining *under*, pin into position to achieve a clean fold at the corner. Using a small circular needle and strong thread, slip-stitch from top to bottom.

Base lining should now be tacked stretched taut across open base of box, spacing tacks approximately 4 cm ($1\frac{1}{2}$ in). Hardboard should be nailed in position over this with edges flush with outside line.

Outside covering may now be smoothed down with a layer of fibre-fill or ample wadding under, to give a padded appearance. This covering should be tacked on the underside, over the edges of the base hardboard. Covering at top corners should be folded under, making a mitre join from inside to outside corners. Joins down corners of box should be slip-stitched. Base of box should be neatened with lining tacked around the four sides.

The piece of hardboard intended for the lid should be nailed into place. At this stage it is advisable to drill holes in lid and box for hinge screws. Foam should now be stuck to the hardboard on the upper face of the lid. Covering should then be laid over the surface of the foam and wrapped down each side and tacked on the underside of the lid. Covering should *not* be tensioned too tightly; just having slackness eased out is sufficient. Pleated corners of the lid should be slip-stitched, finally tacking lining neatly on the base of the lid before screwing hinges in position.

To prevent the lid from opening too wide and straining the hinges, a small length of chain can be fixed inside the box and attached to the lid. Glides or feet may be fixed to the base of the pouffe.

Box pouffe example (*Figure 69*)

A larger box pouffe is shown in figure 69. This has a different construction from the previous example which was made from 12 mm ($\frac{1}{2}$ in) chipboard with sides and base screwed together. The upholstery of the lid can be done in various different ways.

Cover cutting plan is shown in figure 70b.

MATERIALS

Chipboard   12 mm ($\frac{1}{2}$ in) thickness
2 pieces 43 cm × 20 cm (17 in × $7\frac{1}{2}$ in)
2 pieces 40.5 cm × 20 cm (16 in × $7\frac{1}{2}$ in)
2 pieces 43 cm × 43 cm (17 in × 17 in)

Covering	1 m ($1\frac{1}{4}$ yds)
Lining	1 m ($1\frac{1}{4}$ yds)
Foam	46 cm × 46 cm (18 in × 18 in) × 7.5 cm (3 in)
Fibre-fill	1.50 m ($1\frac{3}{4}$ yds) or wadding 2 m (2 yds)
Tacks	10 mm ($\frac{3}{8}$ in) or staples

Construction of box

With the chipboard pieces cut to size, drill holes for screws as shown in figure 69 (also in the edges of the boards). Screw four sides together ensuring that the box is square. It is advisable to pin a temporary stay across two corners whilst the initial work is in progress. Do not screw base on at this stage.

Covering

Cut pieces of lining slightly oversize for the 4 inner surfaces of the box. Using 10 mm ($\frac{3}{8}$ in) fine tacks, work one side at a time and tack lining along narrow top edge of board carefully to avoid damage to edge of board. Smooth lining down and tack opposite side of lining to underside edge of board as at top. After completing one face, work the opposite face. The ends can be held with three or four tacks into the adjacent side. Treat all sides likewise except that the ends of the lining on the two last sides should be folded under, held in position with pins and slip-stitched. It is easier to sew the inner corners at this stage before the bottom is fixed in position.

Lining cut for the bottom should be lightly tensioned across in both directions as it is tacked across the open base. It should be tacked on the edges of the boards on the four sides. With the base lining tacked in position, the baseboard may now be screwed into position. No tacks should be visible in the interior.

Working now with the outside covering cut for the sides, with the box resting on one of its sides, 'back-tack' (*figure 72*) covering along top inside edge of one long side with face side of covering lying on the interior. First put in three or four tacks to hold the material and then with a strip of stout card 1 cm ($\frac{3}{8}$ in) wide, tack over the covering edge with the card flush with the top inside edge. Tacking should be spaced approximately 1 cm ($\frac{3}{8}$ in) keeping tacks close to the edge to prevent the covering pulling up the edge of card. Turning the box over, lay fibre-fill or wadding along the side being covered, smooth the covering over the padding and firstly temporary tack and finally tack 'home' the covering on the

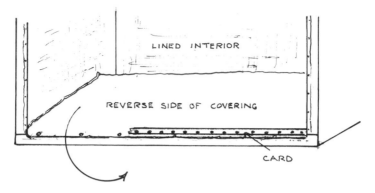

LINED INTERIOR

REVERSE SIDE OF COVERING

CARD

72. 'Back' tacking covering on box lid interior

underside. Ends should be taken around the corner and tacked.

With the first side completed, treat the opposite side in a similar manner and then the remaining two sides. The ends of these should be folded under, pinned into place, then slip-stitched. Should the covering be plastic-coated, decorative nails should be used instead of slip-stitching.

A bottoming of matching lining should be tacked around the outer edges on the underside of the box. Hinges, glides or feet may now be fitted.

Upholstery of lid

Method 1: Wrap-over covering
Lay lid base on to the foam and mark around. Cut foam 6 mm ($\frac{1}{4}$ in) oversize on all sides. Apply adhesive to base in a band of about 5 cm (2 in) along each side, press foam down well to ensure good adhesion; allow to set.

Mark the centre on covering and lid, position covering on to foam, smooth covering down each side, and temporary tack on the underside of lid base. Cover should *not* be tensioned too tightly as this will distort the foam. Finally tack 'home' with a single folded pleat at each corner, slip-stitched. Apply bottoming lining neatly tacked.

Method 2 – 'Float' buttoned (Figure 73)
Establish positions for buttons on baseboard of lid; drill holes 6 mm ($\frac{1}{4}$ in) through board at these points. Cut foam to size of base

plus 6 mm ($\frac{1}{4}$ in) oversize on all sides. Stick foam to board (ensuring equal overlap on each side), as in Method 1.

With an upholsterer's long needle and strong twine, thread twine with needle through wire loop of covered button (or through linen tuft at back of button). Then with two ends of twine threaded

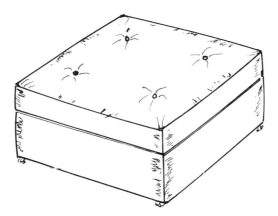

73. 'Float' buttoning of lid

in the needle pass it through the covering immediately over the appropriate hole through the foam and base. Put each button in position before easing twine down on the underside and tacking twine off to the required depth of button. This process can be reversed working a single twine up from the base, threading the button and passing the twine back again.

Method 3 – Deep diamond buttoning (Figure 74)
Cut foam oversize as in previous examples, then mark button positions on lid base (*figure 69*). Drill 6 mm ($\frac{1}{4}$ in) holes through board at button points; mark through to foam. 12 mm ($\frac{1}{2}$ in) holes should be made in the foam at the positions of the buttons.

These holes can easily be made with a short length of piping sharpened at one end. Resting the foam on a block of wood, hammer the piping through the foam. This should give a clean hole for the button to sink into.

Stick foam to board ensuring both sets of holes coincide.

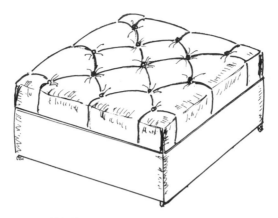

74. Deep diamond buttoning of lid

Covering

Prepare covering; mark centre line in each direction using tailor's chalk on backside of covering. Following these guide lines, mark positions of buttons as on base *with an extra allowance* of 2.8 cm ($1\frac{1}{8}$ in) between each button position, horizontally and vertically (*not* diagonally). The extra allowance between the button positions on the covering will form the diamond shape pleating. There should be pleating around the sides as in figure 74. Buttons should be threaded on to twine and fixed as in float buttoning – in this case the buttons will be eased down rather deeper into the foam. Pleating may be smoothed into position using the handle of a domestic spoon or some such flat object. Folds of pleats should face the same direction.

With the centre buttons tied in, ease covering over the sides, arrange pleats at right angles, tacking covering on the underside. One or two pleats may be used for the corners and these should be 'slip-stitched'.

If desired, fibre-fill may be used under the covering over the foam. This gives a much softer feel and helps the pleating to set into position.

The lid can be neatly finished with matching lining on the underside. Hinges should be fitted and a short thin chain to prevent the lid being opened too wide.

Feet or glides can now be fixed in position.

Television chairs

Figures 75 and 76 show examples of chairs popularly used for watching television. These are sufficiently light to be moved from place to place for best viewing positions.

Chairs used for this purpose generally suffer from over-use, being sat upon for long periods. Consequently, they need replacement or refurbishing rather more frequently than chairs used for other purposes.

EXAMPLE 1 – *Cushion seat with upholstered back*
Cover cutting plan is shown on figure 77**a**.

Figure 75 illustrates frame, cushion and springing and back upholstery, all in sectional drawing. Springing in this instance was 'tension' springing – elongated springs hooked to each side of the seat frame.

A major problem frequently occurs with these springs often through misuse. They become unserviceable through being overstretched, or one of the end hooks may break. Whilst one unserviceable spring may go unnoticed, it may occur with more than one and emergency treatment is then called for. Fortunately, this problem can easily be overcome by replacing the springing with rubber webbing which, in fact, gives far better support to the seat cushion than the 12 mm ($\frac{1}{2}$ in) diameter springs. Firstly, remove the cushion and strip off the covering along the front of seat (and sides if any). Removing the side covering will expose the metal plates holding the springs. All the springs should be unhooked and the side plates unscrewed and completely removed.

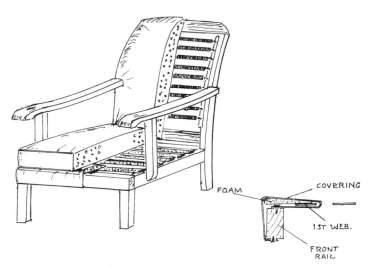

FOAM

COVERING

1ST WEB.

FRONT RAIL

75. TV chair with timber frame

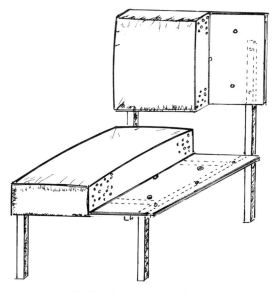

76. TV chair with metal frame

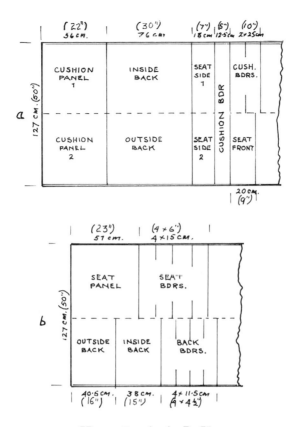

77. **a** cutting plan for Fig 75
b cutting plan for Fig 76 with machined borders

Resilient rubber webbing should be tensioned across the seat using 5 or 6 strands of 5 cm (2 in) width, tensioning at 10% (see pages 32–33). Webbing should be tacked on the top edge of side members (where the metal plates were). The front covering should be taken under the first strand of web, tacked on the top edge of the front rail and brought back over and tacked (*figure 75*).

Generally, when you refurbish a chair of this type, you will find that the back upholstery is still in good condition and only needs recovering. The old covering may be used as a template for cutting the new one. Cushion top or bottom panel can also be used as a template for cutting new panels and borders.

In re-covering the back, the outside back should be stripped off first. If P.V.C., this will be held in place with decorative studs or nails. These can easily be levered out to give access to the tacking of the inside back.

EXAMPLE 2 – *Fixed seat and back (Figure 76)*
Cover cutting plan is shown on figure 77b.

MATERIALS
Foam to fit seat and back (original thickness)
Covering (see cover cutting plan)
Adhesive
10 mm ($\frac{3}{8}$ in) tacks or staples
Bottoming

This type of chair is usually upholstered as two separate seat and back units, both being upholstered on to a baseboard of plywood or other fabricated board and then screwed to the main frame, usually metal.

Seat can be removed by simply removing screws from the underside of the frame. The back unit is normally screwed to the two side upright members under the outside back covering, close to the ends.

To remove back unit, cut stitches or lift out the staples holding the covering – this should reveal the holding screws.

Both units should be removed for the re-covering process or for renewal of foam. Lift out tacks or staples with ripping chisel or screwdriver.

The replacement foam should be of the same depth as originally used for the chair. Strip off foam; do not leave any pieces stuck to the boards. Cut foam 6 mm ($\frac{1}{4}$ in) oversize on all sides, apply adhesive in a band approximately 7.5 cm (3 in) on all sides. Press the foam firmly into position and allow to dry before applying covering.

The simplest method of re-covering both units is by the wrap-over method with covering taken over surface and down sides. The covering for the seat should be tacked or stapled on the underside. Replace bottoming and screw back into position. Covering on back unit should be wrapped from the bottom outside over face, over top border and down outside back, tacking on the bottom edge of board. Sides should be left open to allow for replacement of screws, then pinned down into position and finally slip-stitched.

Should seat and back units be machine seamed at edges the original covering should be taken to pieces to allow the panels and borders to be used as templates for cutting the new covering.

Edges of foam for seat and back will be more stable if they are faced with strips of reconstituted foam 2.5 cm (1 in) thick (*figure 78*) firmly stuck to all face sides. This will reduce the extreme deflection that affects foam at edge pressure points.

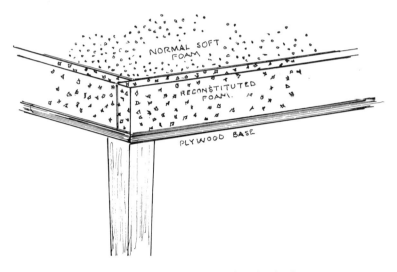

78. Use of reconstituted foam on edge of softer foam

Upholstered bedroom chairs 'pin' stuffed

MATERIALS

    Seat size approximately 38 cm × 35.5 cm (15 in × 14 in)

    Webbing 3 × 2 strands 2 m ($2\frac{1}{4}$ yds)

    Hessian, calico, covering 46 cm × 43 cm (18 in × 15 in)

    Wadding 75 cm ($\frac{3}{4}$ yd)

    Trimming gimp 1.50 m ($1\frac{2}{3}$ yds)

    Adhesive, 10 mm ($\frac{3}{8}$ in) tacks, twine, gimp pins

Upholstery of the Regency style, light and dainty show-wood bedroom chair with what is referred to as 'pin' stuffed upholstery is the most delicate of all upholstering work. These chairs are usually very fragile with very narrow tacking rebates alongside polished surfaces. There is a high risk of damage to the frame and polished finish if suitable care is not taken whilst stripping and upholstering.

Invariably, the common fault needing attention is that the webbing has ripped away from the tacks holding it to the timber of the narrow rebate, causing the surface of the upholstery to sag. To rectify this, a complete strip-down and reupholstering is necessary.

Stripping

Very carefully strip the old materials and filling off, starting with the trimming gimp which will have been stuck into position possibly with a few 'gimp' pins holding the corners.

It is *vitally* important to strip tacks out in the direction of the grain of timber, working from corners towards centres. Damage to the narrow tacking rebate is easily caused by ripping against the grain and a piece of wood missing from the rebate will cause difficulty with re-tacking. In most instances there will be no bottoming fabric on such a seat – occasionally a black linen bottom may be in position below the webbing; this would have been put on as the first item.

Upholstery

When replacing webbing, if the rebate is narrow and shallow, it is advisable to tack webbing single thickness without a fold-over and also to use 10 mm ($\frac{3}{8}$ in) tacks. Ensure that tacks are hammered well 'home'.

Do not use a webbing tool in this instance because of the likelihood that you may damage the frame and polished finish. Tension webbing as tightly as possible by hand.

Hessian should be tacked over webbing; use 10 mm ($\frac{3}{8}$ in) tacks. Both webbing and hessian should be kept well clear of the polished edge alongside the rebate. Sew bridle ties into hessian as shown in figure 37. Tuck filling rather thinly around edges with slight doming towards centre.

Temporary tack lining or calico properly into position over filling, tensioning material towards corners to avoid tack ties (lines caused in material by tack straining too tightly).

Two or three thicknesses of wadding should be laid over the undercover to insulate the filling. Lay covering over wadding, again temporary tack properly into position before finally tacking off. Ensure that hammer face does not hit polished edge. Finally stick trimming gimp alongside polished edge; mitre at corners using gimp pins. Leave temporary tacks in gimp until adhesive has set.

Upholstering 'pin' stuffed seat using foam and rubber webbing

The use of foam and rubber webbing will probably be more attractive to many readers intending to upholster a 'pin' stuffed chair seat (or back), mainly as the materials will be more readily available and possibly easier to work with.

Three strands of 5 cm (2 in) or 4 strands of 4 cm ($1\frac{1}{2}$ in) width rubber webbing should be applied. Space webbing fairly closely, tensioning lightly by hand only. Use 10 mm ($\frac{3}{8}$ in) tacks and ensure that each tack is well 'home'. Trim away surplus webbing clear of rebate polished edge. Figure 79 shows a section through a seat with foam in position and with a fabric strip which has been stuck around the sides and tacked into the rebate to hold the foam in position. The bottom edges of the foam should be bevelled as shown in figure 29.

Covering should be tensioned towards corners while you are temporary tacking and while doing the final tacking in order to avoid tack ties as mentioned in the previous section.

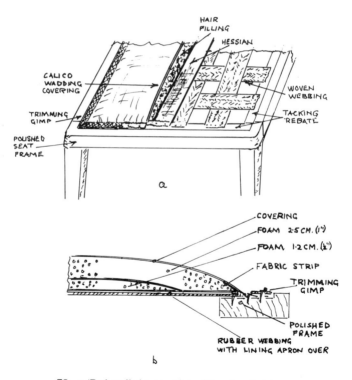

79. **a** 'Pin' stuffed seat with traditional materials
b 'Pin' stuffed seat using rubber webbing, and foam

Upholstered stools

As with other upholstered items, there is a wide variety of upholstered stools available and in popular use ranging from small, low footstools to dressing stools with deep buttoned upholstery.

A number of types using different methods of upholstery are dealt with in this section.

Some stools are very simply padded, for instance, kitchen stools, whilst others for the bedroom or lounge could well be more elaborate to fit in with the decor.

KITCHEN STOOLS

Let us start with the simplest type. Figure 80 shows a simple, practical kitchen stool. Invariably these stools have a plastic covering, with the top and undercovering being heat-sealed around the edge join, thus completely sealing in the baseboard and foam filling with no tacking or stapling.

The top surface covering of the stool may get torn. Although these stools are not very expensive to buy, it is a pity to discard an otherwise sound stool when all it needs is a minor repair as explained below:

Release the seat from the metal base by taking out the holding screws on the underside of the base of seat and cut the plastic covering away. With a newly purchased piece of plastic-coated fabric from the local D.I.Y. store, cut to fit the seat board allowing for a fold-under of approximately 3.5 cm ($1\frac{1}{2}$ in). Should the foam need replacing, the old foam should be cleaned away and the new foam laid in its place with sufficient to pad the extreme edges. Using 10 mm ($\frac{3}{8}$ in) tacks, tack material to underside of seat board. The same material may be tacked on the underside, being folded under whilst being tacked. The seat may then be screwed back into position.

CIRCULAR KITCHEN/BAR STOOL (*Figure 81*)

The covering of this stool may also have been welded around as in the above example with the top edge being formed into an imitation piping. To renew the covering for this circular stool seat, we will need the use of a sewing machine capable of sewing the material chosen. Check beforehand, using either a plain seamed edge or an edge with piping.

The stool top should be unscrewed from the base. Cut away the original covering, or remove tacks if these have been used. Replace foam if needed. A good firm density foam should be used. Using the base board as a template, cut the foam approximately 6 mm ($\frac{1}{4}$ in) oversize and stick it to the board. A firmer edge will be obtained using reconstituted foam as reinforcement

80. Kitchen stool   81. Circular kitchen/bar stool

(*figure 78*). Using the baseboard again as a template, mark around on to reverse side of covering allowing an extra 1 cm ($\frac{1}{2}$ in) for the final cutting line. Cut border; allow an extra 1 cm ($\frac{1}{2}$ in) for the seaming, and an extra 2.5 cm (1 in) fold-under for tacking.

Should a piping be used in the seam, it is essential that strips for making the piping should be cut on the bias; one or two joins in the side border can be made. It is advisable to pin the top panel to the border first to ensure a good fit around the base; should the border be machined too tightly there is a possibility of its splitting.

The sewn covering should be tacked on the underside using 10 mm ($\frac{3}{8}$ in) tacks or staples.

FOOTSTOOLS

Figures 82 and 83 show two footstool frames with simple construction and minimal upholstery.

EXAMPLE A (*Figure 83*)

MATERIALS

> Chipboard 30 cm × 25 cm × 12 mm (12 in × 10 in × $\frac{1}{2}$ in)
>
> Side rails (hard or soft wood) 1.10 m × 48 mm × 23 mm (43 in × 1-$\frac{7}{8}$ in × $\frac{7}{8}$ in)
>
> Edge beading 1.15 m (45 in)
>
> 1 set cabriole legs 15 cm or 20 cm (6 in or 8 in)
>
> Foam 1 piece 30.5 cm × 25.5 cm × 4 cm (12 in × 10 in × 1$\frac{1}{2}$ in)
>
> 1 piece 35 cm × 30 cm × 12 mm (18 in × 16 in × $\frac{1}{2}$ in)
>
> Covering 46 cm × 51 cm (18 in × 20 in)
>
> Trimming 1.12 m (1$\frac{1}{4}$ yds)
>
> Adhesive, screws, veneer pins, 10 mm ($\frac{3}{8}$ in) tacks

Making up frame

Cut side rails to fit, glue and screw flush with outside edges of chipboard. Nail and glue edge beading to bottom line of side rails using fine veneer pins; butt mitred corners. Screw cabriole legs flush with corners of rails. Polish before upholstering.

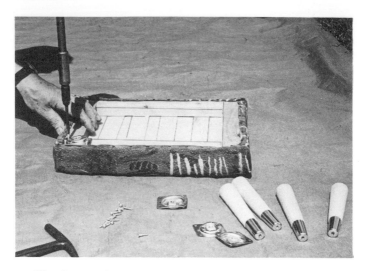

82. Screwing leg plates to underside of footstool   EXAMPLE 'B'

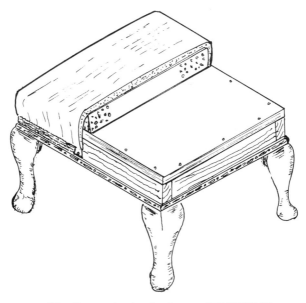

83. Footstool with cabriole egs   EXAMPLE 'A'

Upholstering

Cut thicker foam to size of top board and stick in position. Place thinner foam over surface of first foam, allowing edges to drape half-way down timber sides, lay covering over surface of foam, smooth down sides, temporary tack into position, finally tack home using 10 mm ($\frac{3}{8}$ in) tacks slightly above beading. Trim covering away from beading. Apply trimming using adhesive lightly spread along reverse side (*figure 48*). Temporary tack until adhesive dries, then remove temporary tacks.

EXAMPLE B (*Figure 82 shows leg plates being screwed into position*)

MATERIALS

Hardwood timber 1.10 m × 40 mm × 20 mm (43 in × 1$\frac{1}{2}$ in × $\frac{7}{8}$ in)
10 mm dowel
Rubber webbing 1.20 m (48 in)
Foam 36 cm × 25 cm × 4 cm (14 in × 10 in × 1$\frac{1}{2}$ in)
Covering 56 cm × 46 cm (22 in × 18 in)
4 strips 4 cm (1$\frac{1}{2}$ in) wide linen or calico
Adhesive
10 mm and 13 mm ($\frac{3}{8}$ in and $\frac{1}{2}$ in) tacks

Frame should be made up using dowelled or mortice and tenoned joints, glued and cramped until dry.

4 strands of 4 cm (1$\frac{1}{2}$ in) resilient rubber webbing should be tacked to frame surface using 13 mm ($\frac{1}{2}$ in) tacks, tensioning webbing at 7$\frac{1}{2}$% to 10%.

Foam is now cut 6 mm ($\frac{1}{4}$ in) oversize on all sides, using the frame as a template. Stick strips of lining or calico along foam side edges approximately half-way up sides to leave flanges below bottom of foam.

Laying foam over frame and webbing, tack flanges to edges of frame on all four sides.

Using wrap-over method of covering, lay covering over foam, smooth down sides, temporary tack into position, finally tacking off with covering folded *under* at line of tacking on the underside. Ensure that sufficient space is left at corners for leg plates to be screwed into position. Covering should be finished with a single pleat at corners. Leg plates should be screwed into position so that legs splay outwards.

DRESSING STOOLS

EXAMPLE: *Deep buttoned dressing stool (Figures 84, 85, 86 and 87)*

MATERIALS
>   Chipboard or plywood
>   51 cm × 38 cm × 12 mm (20 in × 15 in × $\frac{1}{2}$ in)
>   1 set 38 cm (15 in) cabriole legs
>   Battening rail (hard or soft wood)
>   1.80 m × 30 mm × 23 mm (72 in × $1\frac{1}{4}$ in × $\frac{7}{8}$ in)
>   Wood screws 5 cm (2 in) × 8 gauge and 2.5 cm (1 in) ×
>   6 gauge
>   Foam 1 piece 51 cm × 38 cm × 4 cm (20 in × 15 in ×
> $1\frac{1}{2}$ in)
>   1 piece 56 cm × 43 cm × 4 cm (22 in × 17 in × $1\frac{1}{2}$ in)
>   Fibre-fill 61 cm × 46 cm (24 in × 18 in) if desired
>   Trimming gimp or fringe 2 m (2 yds)
>   10 Covered upholstery buttons
>   Adhesive for wood
>   Covering 81 cm × 68.5 cm (32 in × 27 in)

Making up frame
Cut chipboard or plywood and side battening to size. Glue and screw cabriole legs in position on baseboard. Glue and screw battening around sides on top surface of baseboard. Screw from underside of board.

Upholstery
Mark positions of buttons on baseboard and drill 6 mm ($\frac{1}{4}$ in) holes at button positions to allow button twines to pass through. Cut the smaller piece of foam to fit within the side rails. Before fitting, mark button positions on both pieces of foam ensuring that marking is centrally placed on both pieces of foam and that the holes will coincide on both pieces when punched through with the

84. Components for dressing stool

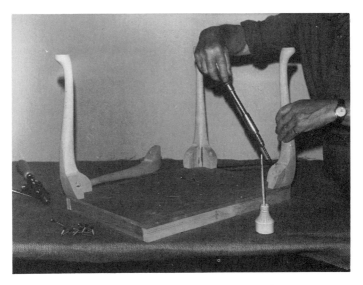

85. Assembling dressing stool

111

86. Dressing stool frame

87. Completed dressing stool

112

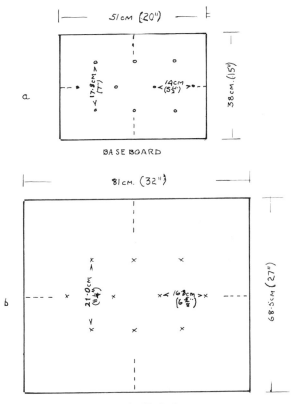

BASE BOARD

COVER MARKING.

88. **a** holes in baseboard for stool

 b button positions on covering

piece of sharpened tube, *see page 95.* Now mark button positions on reverse side of covering with tailor's chalk, working each way from centre lines. The distance between button positions on covering must make allowance for the pleating; you need an extra 1/5th between buttons, i.e. for a length of diamond add 3.2 cm ($1\frac{1}{4}$ in); width of diamond will be 2.8 cm ($1\frac{1}{8}$ in).

Fibre-fill may be used over the foam to give added depth and softness. With the covering laid over the surface of the stool,

113

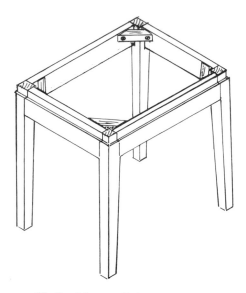

89. Stool frame with dowelled joints

thread strong twine on to a long upholsterer's needle. Pass the twine through the loop or tuft of button and pass the needle through covering at the appropriate point, through the *correct* hole in the foam and through the hole in the base. Ease down lightly and temporary tack on the underside tying the twine temporarily until all the buttons and pleats are in position so that they may then be tied down and tacked at the same level. After buttoning is completed, side pleating should be adjusted so that the folds of pleats run straight and square down the sides. Finish off with a linen or calico bottoming, sticking gimp or fringe around base of the seat above the cabriole legs.

Figure 89 shows a traditional type of framed dressing stool with dowelled joints. This stool frame will allow for the traditional form of coil springing and stuffing, with webbing fixed to the underside of the frame. It may be 'top' stuffed if desired (*see page 53*). As a further option rubber webbing and foam may be used.

Covering may be a plain 'wrap-over' finish or be deeply buttoned as in the previous example.

LIST OF DISTRIBUTORS OF UPHOLSTERY SUNDRIES

U.K.

Aberkenfig Upholstery, 5 Bridgend Road, Aberkenfig, Bridgend, Glam

Acre Furnishing Services Ltd, 38–40 Kennington Park Road, London SE11 4RS

Andrews Upholstery, 302 Oxford Road, Reading, Berks RG3 1ER

Anglia Upholstery (Ipswich) Ltd, Unit 12, Dedham Place Workshops, Water Works Street, Ipswich, Suffolk

Antiques of Tomorrow, 17 Tower Street, Rye, East Sussex TN31 7AU (Polished and unpolished frames and velvet coverings only)

Aquarius Soft Furnishing, 5a Hamilton House, Heath Road, Cox Heath, Maidstone, Kent

C. Atkins, 1 Union Street, Newport Pagnell, Bucks

A. Baker & Son, 71a Fore Street, Ipswich, Suffolk IP4 1JZ

Barking Home Improvements, 350 Ripple Road, Barking, Essex

Barnes & Co (Materials), Kangley Bridge Road, Sydenham, London SE26 5AX

Bedford Upholstery Service, c/o Tina's, 139 Kettering Road, Northampton

David Block, 150 Station Road, Woburn Sands, Milton Keynes, Beds

Bruno-Galetti Ltd, 72 Haverstock Hill, London NW3 2BE

Buxton Upholstery, 5 Scarsdale Place, Buxton, Derbyshire SK17 6EF

Coleman's, 28–30 Market Street, Birkenhead, Cheshire

Conway Furnishers, 3–5 High Street, Dunmow, Essex CM6 1AB

Coventry Foam and Upholstery Supplies, 65–69 Coventry Street, Stoke, Coventry CV2 4ND

Mr. Crumpton, 42 St. Neots Road, Sandy, Beds

P. J. David & Son, 16c Church Street, St. George's, Telford

Dee Cee, 27 Hayburn Road, Millbrook Estate, Southampton, Hants

Dudley Home Interiors, Vine House, Fair Green Reach, Cambridge

The Easy Chair, 30 Lyndhurst Road, Worthing, Sussex

R. Eldridge, 502 Portswood Road, Southampton, Hants SO5 3SA

A. C. Fish, Bullace Lane, r/o 82 High Street, Dartford, Kent

Fourways Furnishings Ltd, 5 Sevenoaks Road, Borough Green, Kent

Fringe & Fabrics, Station Road, Broxbourne, Herts

Gem Upholstery, 157 Southend Road, Grays, Essex RM17 5NP

Gravesham Upholstery, 4–5 East Milton Road, Gravesend, Kent

W. A. V. Hallett (Furn.) & Son, 53 High Street, Lee-on-Solent, Hants PO13 9BU

W. E. Harryman, 145 Half Moon Lane, Herne Hill, London SE24 9JY

S. Hodgson, 36 High Street, Shefford, Beds SG17 5DG

Hornet Hardware, 24 The Hornet, Chichester, West Sussex

J. E. Janes, 32 Clarence Road, Grays, Essex RM17 6QJ

Jonmar Upholstery, The Old Maltings, St. Andrews Street South, Bury St. Edmunds, Suffolk

K. & M. Upholstery, 165 Luckwell Road, Bristol BS3 3HB

Brian Kirby & Co, 154 Springfield Road, Brighton, Sussex BN1 6DG

Local Trading Co, 207 London Road, Sheffield S2 4LJ

Lowcross, 33 High Street, Whitchurch, Shropshire

D. M. McCartney (Furnishing), 1 Mansfield Road, Baldock, Herts SG7 6EB

W. Monks & Sons, London Road, Sawbridgeworth, Herts

Morgan Handyman Supplies, 27 Carlton Road, Nottingham, Notts

N. R. Neve, 31 The Broadway, St. Ives, Hunts PE17 4BX

A. C. Prickett & Sons Ltd, 42 The Broadway, Leigh-on-Sea, Essex

F. E. Puleston Co Ltd, r/o 148 Leagrave Road, Luton, Beds

R. D. Upholstery, 26 Elm Parade, Elm Park, Essex

Re-Upholstery (Mr. Flood), Trafalgar Street, Gillingham, Kent

A. J. Roberts & Co Ltd, 8 Tudor Road, Cardiff CF1 8RF

Russell Trading Co, 75 Paradise Street, Liverpool L1 3BP

J. P. Shearn, 9 Park Place, Dover, Kent

Mr. A. Smith, 5a High Street, Hadleigh, Suffolk

Strand Upholstery, 793 Southchurch Road, Southend-on-Sea, Essex

Superease Upholstery, 5 Hannah Street North, Rhondda, Glam

I. R. Taylor, 12 Malpas Road, Newport, Gwent NPT 5PA

F. W. Tuck, Russells Yard, Bell Street, Great Baddow, Essex

F. H. Watts Ltd, The Handyman Centre, 111 Shirley Road, Southampton, Hants

H. D. Winslow, 460 London Road, Westcliff-on-Sea, Essex SS0 9LA

Yeovil Upholsteries D.I.Y. Supply Centre, 9 Wyndham Street, Yeovil, Somerset

GLOSSARY

Alva Marino Dried seaweed used as an upholstery filling during the Victorian period

Back-tacking A method of attaching covering to hide tacks

Bayonet needle Long upholstery needle with triangular point

Bevelled edge Removal of sharp edge of timber rail (*see* chamfer)

Bias cutting Cutting fabric diagonally across threads at 45 degrees

Blind stitch Stitches forming loops within the filling to consolidate the edge

Bottoming Material tacked on the underside of upholstered work for a neat finish

Bridle ties Loops of twine sewn into hessian to hold filling in place

Cabriole leg Queen Anne style leg

Calico A white cotton material used as undercovering for upholstery work

Canvas Coarse cloth woven from jute fibre used to support filling and cover springs (*see* hessian)

Chamfer Bevel on corner edge of timber

Chipboard Fabricated board made from wood chips

Chip foam Firm foam made from granulated waste polyether foam (reconstituted foam)

Coil spring Traditional type of upholstery spring

Creep Movement of upholstery filling during use

Deflection Reduction of depth of filling caused by pressure

Density Relating to quality of foam

DIY Do-it-yourself amateur handicraft work

Diamond buttoning Deep buttoning of upholstery causing pleats to form into diamond formation

Doming Degree of rise in centre of seat or cushion

Dowelled joint Timber joint held together with wooden pegs and glue

'Drop-in' seat Loose seat to fit into rebate of dining chair or bedroom stool

Fibre Coarse filling used for the 'first' stuffing of upholstery

Fibre-fill Soft filling made from terylene fibre

Fine needle Long slender needle used for upholstery buttoning

Fine tacks Slender tacks used for light timber

Float buttoning Covered buttons lightly sunk into covering

Fringe Decorative trimming placed around the base of upholstered items

Fullness Surplus covering causing wrinkling

Gimp Narrow decorative band to hide tacks along a rebate

Gimp pins Very fine tacks with small heads, available in various colours

Groundwork Basic working at the commencement of buttoning

Hardwood Close-grained timber suitable for upholstery frames

Hassocks Firm kneeling cushions

Hessian Coarse cloth woven from jute fibre (*see* canvas)

Hide pincers Wide-jawed pincers for tensioning leather

Horsehair Good quality filling for traditional upholstery. Often mixed with pig hair

Improved tacks Tacks with thicker shanks and larger heads than the fine version

Jute A coarse fibre used in the weaving of hessian and some webbing

Laid-cord Thick spring lashing cord make from flax or hemp fibre

Latex foam Upholstery foam manufactured from sap of rubber tree

Leather cloth Upholstery covering used mainly in the Victorian period to imitate leather

Linen webbing Good quality webbing woven from flax and cotton fibres

Lining A thin cotton fabric of various colours

Mattress stitch Looped stitches around borders of mattresses and squab cushions

Mitred Joined diagonally

Molegrips Specialised type of pliers

Mortice Slot cut into timber to house tenon

No-sag Proprietary type of modern springing

Oxidised nails Domed decorative nails with oxidised finish

Pincore latex Latex foam moulded with pencil-like holes through its depth

Pin-stuffed An upholstered seat using one layer of filling only

Piping Decoration to camouflage a machined seam

Polyether foam Flexible foam produced by mixture of chemicals

Pouffe Floor cushion generally made for fireside use

Prefabricated board Sheet of wood made mechanically

PVC Polyvinyl chloride covering

Radius section Part of frame with curved section

Rasp Coarse file for timber

Rebate A recess machined in timber frame for tacking of covering

Reconstituted foam (*See* chip foam)

Refurbishing Restoring

Regulate To use regulator

Regulator An upholsterer's needle with flat end

Resilient webbing Laminated rubber webbing

Resiliency Amount of flexibility or springiness

Ruche Decorative trimming to hide machine join in covering

Sash cramp Long bar with adjustable jaws to hold timber after gluing

Scrim Loosely-woven material to encase filling for stitching rolls on seats, etc.

Second stuffing Stuffing, generally of a better quality, worked over the 'first' stuffing

Stile A member in the construction of the frame interfering with the tuck through of covering

Show-wood frame An upholstered frame with a large amount of polished wood visible

Sinuous spring Modern type of springing consisting of continuous length of wire formed into 'U' shapes

Slip knot   A knot made in a length of twine which will 'slip' tight

Slip-stitching   Method of 'closing' joins in covering fabric on the job

Spring needle   Thick curved needle

Squab   Flat cushion generally firmly filled

Tack-roll   A method of softening a timber rail around the edge of seat, etc.

Tack ties   Strain lines across fabric caused by tack straining fabric

Teasing   Opening of stuffing by working with fingers

Template   A paper or card shape used for accurate cutting of covering

Temporary tacking   The initial tacking process leaving tacks protruding

Tenon   The projecting piece

Tension spring   An elongated small diameter coil spring fixed at ends

Thumb-roll   Tack-roll approximately the thickness of the thumb

Top stitch   The final row of stitching to obtain a 'fine' edge

Top-stuffed   Upholstery worked on the top surface of seat members

Wood-wool   Shredded wood fibres

Zig-Zag springing   A proprietary form of sinuous spring formed from a series of 'U' bends

Index